"Reflect upon your present blessings, of which
every man has plenty; not on your past misfortunes,
of which all men have some."

—CHARLES DICKENS

WHISTLE STOP
Café
MYSTERIES

# STAIRWAY
# to the STARS

## RUTH LOGAN HERNE

Cover and interior design by Müllerhaus
Cover illustration by Greg Copeland at Illustration Online LLC.
Typeset by Aptara, Inc.

ISBN 978-1-961251-40-3 (hardcover)
ISBN 978-1-961251-41-0 (epub)

Printed and bound in the United States of America
10 9 8 7 6 5 4 3 2 1

# STAIRWAY
## to the STARS

# CHAPTER ONE

Janet Shaw took a deep breath of crisp autumn air and paused long enough to enjoy the clear blue sky. There was nothing like a bright fall day.

"These rolls smell divine." Debbie Albright lifted the box of eight pumpkin rolls from the back of Janet's car and set it atop the first box she'd brought out. That one was filled with chocolate cake rolls, another crowd-pleasing favorite at the depot and Claymont Creek Farm. "I'm so hungry, I could sit down and eat one myself. It's a good thing there are no forks handy."

"That's what happens when you save your appetite for dinner with a cute guy." Janet winked at her longtime best friend and current business partner. Almost a year and a half ago they'd opened a café and bakery in the old train depot, and neither one regretted a moment of their new endeavor. "Who'd have thought high school football could take on such a level of importance?"

Debbie laughed as Janet eased out a plastic tote. This one was filled with pecan pies, neatly packaged in perfectly sized pastry boxes, ready for sale at the farm. The farm's ovens had broken the previous day. After a panicked call from Dani Addison, their old friend and classmate, Janet and Debbie had jumped in to help fill the farm's bakery case prior to a busy fall weekend.

"Jaxon being named to the Division IV Regional team means dinner tonight is a family celebration. We'll have both boys and Greg's mom. To misquote an old baseball axiom: There *is* joy in Mudville tonight. Getting that recognition as a sophomore is pretty amazing."

"It's well deserved after the season they had." Janet raised a brow as she lifted her totes. "We've had some rough ones lately. Plus, who knows what Jaxon's junior year will bring?"

"This isn't a path I would have expected eighteen months back, but it's a path I'm loving now," Debbie replied. "Is this all?" She jutted her chin at their bounty of baked goods.

"For the moment. This will help get Dani through tomorrow at least. What a rough time of year to have her big oven go down." Janet led the way into the attractive farm store owned by the Addisons.

They'd no sooner gotten through the door than Dani was there to greet them.

"Janet, Debbie, I don't know how to thank you!" Dani hurried forward, with her mother, Agnes, right behind her. "When that oven died, I went into panic mode. There's too much going on this month to have my oven break down." She took a tote from Debbie, and Agnes took one from Janet. "This is make-it-or-break-it time in farm sales. These three months are where we stay in business or fold up our tents."

Her mother rolled her eyes, giving Janet and Debbie a knowing, patient smile.

Dani backtracked slightly. "Okay, we won't really roll up the tents, but fourth-quarter sales are crucial. Janet, you're a lifesaver."

"Happy to help," Janet told her as they applied the farm's custom labels to the products. Dani had run the other packaging materials over to Janet the previous day. Janet's mother had jumped in to help, and between their home ovens as well as the Addisons', they'd been able to whip up a solid number of baked goods.

But with the weekend upon them, it wasn't quite enough. The Addisons' Claymont Creek Farm was a destination for many people in the fall and winter. The farm offered plenty of other activities throughout the year, such as strawberry and raspberry picking, and people loved to stop by and bring tiny treats to the Addisons' fleet of miniature donkeys. Still, the farm's busiest season was September through December. The main oven breaking down was one of the worst things that could happen this time of year.

"Paulette and Debbie ran the café to give me extra baking time," Janet explained as they moved toward the quaint bakery area of the farm store. "Any word on repairs?"

"The service provider was here yesterday afternoon," said Dani.

"That's good, right?" Janet asked.

But Dani's expression was grim. "Not so much. The ignitor is bad, and there are none in stock in the area. The new one won't arrive until Monday, which means an entire weekend—the second weekend of November, no less—of blank shelves."

"I'll jump on whatever you'd like tonight," Janet told her. "I can repeat today's offerings or move to cookies or cupcakes. Or muffins. You know my pumpkin muffins are a great seller."

Dani laughed. "They sure are. Since you shared your recipe with me, I've barely been able to keep them in stock. They positively fly off the shelves."

"I'm glad to hear it." Janet slapped the final sticker on a pecan pie and nudged Dani's shoulder. "That's what friends are for, isn't it?"

"At least baking friends," Debbie teased. "I'm happy to carry things and take care of customers with Paulette, but apart from the occasional cupcake, not much goes on in my oven, and I'm okay with that."

"Let it never be said that delivery service is overrated," Dani said. "You guys want coffee? Or hot cider?"

"Hot cider sounds wonderful." Janet accepted a box of packaging from Agnes and moved to the door. "I'll put these in the car."

At the car, she sent her husband, Ian, a quick text. She doubted he would have time for a call, as he was likely having a busy day as Dennison's chief of police, but he still appreciated when she checked in. Dropping off the baked goods to Claymont Creek Farm and having cider with Dani. Home soon.

Ian sent back, Sounds good. Tell Dani we're checking out the broken fencing by the donkey exhibit. I'll call her tomorrow with an update.

Will do. Janet went back inside. The inviting scent of hot spiced apples filled the air. She inhaled deeply. "That smell is intoxicating, isn't it?"

"There's nothing like it on a cool fall day," Debbie agreed.

"I'm still in love with the scent of spiced cider, even after all this time," Dani said. "It gives such a sense of contentment. No matter where you are, that scent feels like home."

"It does," Janet agreed. "And Ian said to tell you that he'll be in touch tomorrow about your fencing issue. Is that something you want to talk about?"

Dani's expression shadowed. "It seems someone deliberately cut the perimeter fence on the miniature donkey pen. Dad was doing a check this morning and found one of the eight-foot sections sliced open."

"Like someone actually cut the fencing?" Janet stopped with her cider halfway to her lips. "On purpose? Why would someone want to do that?"

"That's why we called the police station," Agnes said. "We can't imagine who would do such a thing, but it doesn't appear to be an accident."

"How can you tell?" Debbie asked.

"If a car or something had hit the fence, it would damage the post and bow the fencing. That wasn't the case," Agnes explained. "The fence wasn't bent in, and the posts are fine. That fence was cut, like with wire cutters or something similar, neat as can be. The saving grace was that the fencing snagged on one of the metal loops we put in for reinforcement at the bottom, and the donkeys didn't notice the breach. If they had, we'd have had donkeys in the road and the fields or gorging themselves on apples."

"Who would do such a thing?" Debbie asked. "That's crazy."

Dani frowned. "Unfortunately, it's one of half a dozen things that have gone wrong in the past few weeks. Not enough to spell catastrophe, but enough to put us behind every weekend. The trusty tractor that Dad painstakingly maintains wouldn't start last weekend, and that messed up our hayrides on Saturday. It wasn't anything major, thank heavens. But I can't figure out how a tractor that's treated as well as ours ended up with bad gasoline."

"And not having the hayrides got us a couple of low reviews online," Agnes added. "We never get bad reviews. We pride ourselves on keeping people happy."

Janet was well aware. The farm's whole philosophy was to give their customers a magical, affordable, family-friendly experience. Because of that, hundreds of people came to the farm each weekend during the last four months of the year.

"You guys run an amazing operation here," Janet said. "And you've blessed several generations already. That's pretty great." Janet's and Debbie's parents had brought them to the farm as children. Ian and Janet had done the same with Tiffany and her friends. Autumn at Claymont Creek Farm had become a Dennison tradition.

"It gets tiring after a while." Agnes stood and laid a hand on her daughter's shoulder. "I need to get supper going for your dad. It's too dark for him to do much now, but you know how he is. The shorter days of November and December stress him out. He never feels like he's on top of things these two months, even though he's always overprepared. Good to see you, ladies, and thank you so much for the help." She left through the back door, stepping into the yard between the barn that had been converted to a shop and the old farmhouse.

When the door closed behind her mother, Dani leaned forward and rested her head in her hands.

"Dani, what's going on?" Janet came around the table and took the seat next to her old friend. She had a feeling that there was even more than Agnes knew.

"I don't know." Dani straightened then twisted her hands in her lap. "The log splitter that Dad uses all winter to take care of firewood for customers has disappeared. We're not sure when it went missing because we're too busy this time of year to split wood, but he went out to the woodpile three weeks back and discovered that it was gone. Someone must have driven back there, hooked it up, and rolled away with it, and we have no idea who or when except that Dad was using it the third week of September."

"That's no small thing," Debbie said. "I wonder how someone pulled that off."

"We kept it behind the old barn," Dani explained. "That way it's separated from the action up here. Being out of sight and out of mind, none of us had a clue it was gone. Of course we reported it to Ian, but I'm sure the time lapse left him little to go on. Since we don't know when it was taken, any evidence that might have been there will be long gone."

"That's probably true," Janet said regretfully.

"Then the plumbing in the small barn—the square building out back with two bathrooms—went bad a couple weeks ago. We tried all the normal fixes to get things up and running again, but nothing worked. We had to have someone come and dig up the piping to the septic, and they found that it was plugged with coconut oil." She tapped the table in exasperation. "Solidly plugged."

"That's a nasty situation," Debbie said. "How did the coconut oil get there?"

Dani's frown intensified. "Your guess is as good as mine, but it's not as if it could have happened on accident. Who puts coconut oil down a bathroom drain or a toilet? They had to cut through the pipes with a saw. Thank heavens the baking area has its own piping to the house septic system so the clog didn't affect us here, but we had to pay to have three portable restrooms brought in and to have the restroom plumbing repaired. It was dreadful. And expensive."

Tiny hairs raised along Janet's neck. She locked eyes with Debbie and saw a similar concern in her friend's gaze. "Dani, I hate to say this, but I think the answer to your question—the one about who puts coconut oil down a bathroom drain—is easy. Because no one would do that unless they meant to block the pipes. It's starting to sound like a pattern to me."

Dani stared at Janet. "You think someone may be trying to sabotage the farm?"

Janet ticked off examples on her fingers. "Stolen equipment, fouled gas, cut fencing, blocked pipes, and now a bad ignitor on your oven? I'm just saying that's a lot of coincidences in a mighty short period of time."

Dani sat back with a slight thump. "I can't deny that I've been wondering about that too, but I kept telling myself it wasn't possible because I couldn't think of why anyone would want to do that. Mom and Dad have been talking about retirement, so they see these things as signs that maybe that's exactly what they should do. They know I want to keep the farm running, but I don't know how I could do it alone. My brother isn't interested in it, but technically he and I share ownership."

Janet remained quiet, sensing that her friend needed to talk it out.

Dani grimaced. "I'd have to make payments to my brother to buy out his share. I can't just step in and take ownership. That part's okay, but having so many things going wrong at once is unnerving. Developers are circling this whole area like vultures, grabbing properties as soon as they become available. Land around here has become a valuable commodity. Maybe I should give it up while prices are so high. Perhaps it's God's way of telling me that it's time to let go. Except I feel in my heart that I'm supposed to run this farm, and if it was God's timing, I don't think I'd feel that way, right?"

"It could be that someone is giving you a warning for selfish, human reasons, which feels more likely to me," Janet told her. "I'm a firm believer in God's timing, but I don't think He's behind a slew of equipment problems."

"Me either," Debbie agreed. "Two is a coincidence. Five distinct problems in a well-kept establishment, including cut wire and fouled gas, send up red flags in my brain." She set her mug down and leaned forward. "Doesn't it seem weird that all this is happening right when your parents are talking about retirement and you're considering taking over the farm?"

Dani's eyebrows rose. "I hadn't thought of it that way. It's been too busy for me to sit back and analyze things, but yes. It is weird. And at a time when I felt like life was definitely improving. But who would do something like this? Who would have the inner ugliness to try to hurt a small family farm?"

Janet and Debbie exchanged glances. When Debbie gave a slight nod, Janet covered Dani's hand with one of her own. "I don't know, Dani. But we'd sure like a chance to find out."

# CHAPTER TWO

Janet spent the whole night baking. She restocked the café's inventory first then took another carload of things to Claymont Creek Farm at seven the following morning.

Dani helped her carry the totes in then threw her arms around Janet in a big hug. "I can't tell you how grateful I am. Between what you've brought, what I did at our house last night, and my freezer stash, we should be fine. This puts me in a much better position than I was twenty-four hours ago. You really stayed up all night?"

Janet patted her back then released her. "Reminded me of holiday prep over on Third Street, and how glad I am that we're not that big because I do like my sleep." She grinned at Dani as they carried the final totes into the quaint sales barn. "It is invigorating to do this now and again, but I'm looking forward to a nice nap in about thirty minutes. When you get through this weekend, Debbie and I want to figure out what's happening over here. If that's all right with you, of course."

"I would appreciate that, but it has to be done quietly because I don't want to alarm my parents," Dani replied. "Dad especially. He's a great guy, but you know how he is. He'll refuse to acknowledge it, but he'll still stress about it and bottle it up."

"I remember." Dani's dad, Clint, was a good and kind man, but undeniably stuck in his ways. "He stands his ground."

"That's a nice way of saying 'stubborn beyond all reason.'" Dani filled the left side of the farm bakery case while Janet stocked the near side. "It's not one of his best traits. He's completely resistant to any new ideas in farming and production, but since his ways have worked for decades, who am I to argue? Although I'm glad the stubborn gene skipped me."

"How about if Debbie and I stop by Monday after we close the café?" Janet stacked the now-empty totes then set the tops inside. "Maybe we can have a look around."

"Tuesday, instead?" Dani suggested. "Dad has a dental appointment Tuesday afternoon. He'd never schedule an appointment during our busy time under normal circumstances, but he's got a bad molar that's leaving him little choice."

"Tooth pain can be awful. Tuesday afternoon, then. I'll text when we're on our way."

"Perfect."

Janet headed home and caught a three-hour nap before heading to the Whistle Stop Café. She parked in the public lot and couldn't hold back a smile as she climbed out of the car and spotted the skating rink between the town's historic memorial and the Grant Street gazebo. Tiffany and her friends had enjoyed the rink several times over Christmas break in years past.

On the opposite side of the parking area was the historic Dennison Railroad Depot and Museum. The iconic depot had provided comfort and refreshments for tens of thousands of World War II troops as they headed off to the front. Dennison had earned the nickname "Dreamsville, USA" during the war because of the warm hospitality provided by the thousands of Salvation Army volunteers, no matter what time of day the soldiers rolled through. People would stream to the depot laden with cakes, cookies, sandwiches, coffee, lemonade, cider, and more. They shared whatever they had on hand with the service personnel who came through town. A dedicated Salvation Army kiosk had been staffed by women who fried their famous doughnuts to be handed out to the troops.

And there, on the west end of the renovated depot, was the Whistle Stop Café.

Paulette waved in welcome as Janet walked in the door before she resumed taking a table's order. Paulette Connor had come on board at the café shortly after they opened. It hadn't taken Janet and Debbie long to realize they needed an extra set of hands, at least part-time. Paulette was friendly and efficient, the perfect addition to their staff.

She had the handful of tables well in hand, and while the bakery case wasn't full, they had plenty to get through a morning of walk-ins and orders.

Janet poked her head into the kitchen to let Debbie know she'd arrived. "Good morning."

"Nice to see you. How'd your baking marathon go?" Debbie filled wraps with her ever-popular chicken salad then topped them with a smattering of chopped walnuts and dried cranberries before wrapping them neatly. "Is Dani better?"

"I think they've got enough stock for a busy fall weekend. I told her we'd meet up on Tuesday to see if we can get a handle on things. Does that work for you?"

"No problem," Debbie agreed.

"I want to go through our supplies and figure out what we're short of, but did you need me to refill anything in the display case first?"

Debbie gestured to a sheet pan rack that still held a few trays of baked goods. "We're all set for now."

"Great. Let me know if anything comes up." Janet hung up her hooded sweatshirt then took down her clipboard to begin a checklist for ordering supplies, starting up front. There was no such thing as too much during the busy holiday baking season.

She paused as Jim Watson, the local newspaper editor, stepped inside. He greeted a good share of the customers at the tables then took a seat on one of the stools. "Busy as usual, eh? And a new T-shirt, I see."

Janet's baking-themed T-shirts were well-known around town. Today's selection featured pumpkin graphics and fall colors with the words BAKING IS LOVE MADE EDIBLE. "I couldn't resist. Your usual?"

"Yes please."

Her phone pinged with a text from depot museum curator Kim Smith. ON MY WAY. COULD YOU HAVE A SIXTEEN-OUNCE REGULAR COFFEE AND A TWENTY-OUNCE EXTRA-HOT MOCHA READY FOR ME WHEN I GET THERE?

Janet texted back a confirmation then shifted to the coffee machine to get Jim's coffee and make Kim's order.

Debbie emerged from the kitchen with an order and read the new T-shirt slogan with a grin. "The new shirt is perfect, Janet."

"I'm glad you like it." Janet slid Jim's coffee in front of him then started Kim's order. "Jim, busy has become the understatement of the year. We are blessed, for sure. The accident of good timing."

Jim disagreed. "It's no accident. Great owners, great product, and smart management. With the push toward future development in Dennison and Uhrichsville, you made the move at the right time.

Property prices are rising as more people want to move into the area. Who'd have thought of our village as a 'destination point' for young families? But that's what they're calling it now, and the numbers back it up. I'm just hoping we don't grow so prosperous that it raises the cost of living for our older population. Many of them live on fixed incomes."

"That's a good point, Jim." Janet handed him a miniature pitcher of half-and-half. "Do you see that becoming a problem?"

"It's a possibility but not a guarantee," he told her.

"I heard this year's kindergarten class is much bigger than last year's," Debbie said on her return to the counter from delivering her order. "With new neighborhoods being developed, they expect those numbers to keep climbing. What can I get you to eat, Jim?"

"Tuna on grilled rye, with a dash of dill?"

"Coming right up." She flashed him a smile before going back to the cooking area.

"Those kindergarten numbers will keep climbing right along with our taxes!" Troy Henry grumbled the words as he met Paulette at the cash register.

Troy's family had lived in the area for several generations. At an age when most men would be retired, Troy still managed several local properties, including individual storage units in an old warehouse building. He was a bit of a curmudgeon, but the man could smell a good deal a mile away, and he'd made a decent living from that skill. He didn't part with money easily or suffer fools readily, and it was clear he was on a roll today.

"Those of us who invested in this town when it was struggling to make ends meet don't need our taxes hiked for some fancy light poles hung with doodads that don't mean a thing. It's not as if there's a stream of people driving up and down Grant Street to see the sights."

Paulette gave him his change. "Troy, I hear you loud and clear, but those pretty hanging baskets, all filled with flowers grown right here in Dennison, always make me smile. Winter comes soon enough. Things lie fallow a good while. I say we cheer on the flowers and good wishes while we can."

Troy huffed, but he regularly used Greg Connor for renovation work on his multiple properties. He wasn't likely to offend Greg's mother.

Janet stifled a chuckle.

Troy headed out the front door, passing Kim Smith on her way inside for her coffee order.

"Almost done," Janet told her. "How are Christmas Train ticket sales going?"

"We're selling tickets like hotcakes as usual." Kim took a seat next to Jim. "Your coverage in the *Gazette* is always a help, Jim. Thank you."

"Happy to do it. Keeping this depot in the news is something we take seriously down at the paper. Not many small towns have something as historic as the Dennison Depot to shout about. We're lucky to have it and to have you in charge. You've made a difference, Kim. In lots of ways."

"Thank you. I'm so glad to hear when people are pleased with my work." The praise made her beam. "The downside is that it's hard to schedule in proper family time for Thanksgiving because we're so busy here. I wanted to get my family together for a big Thanksgiving gathering. Mom's age makes every holiday one to remember, but I keep running into timing snags with my siblings and their families. It seems the logistics aren't in my favor."

Kim's mother was Eileen Palmer. She'd run the busy depot at age twenty during World War II. With her over a hundred years old, her family treasured every moment they had with her.

"That's a tough travel week in a lot of ways." Debbie set Jim's plate of food before him. "And with all the flight delays lately, it's hard to plan an event with people traveling in from multiple places, even something as simple as a meal, and get everyone together on time."

Kim nodded agreement. "That's it exactly. Some have commitments to spouse's families, and others don't have enough time off from school to make the trip feasible. So my great idea of gathering everyone together to have a perfect Thanksgiving has pretty much blown up in my face. Remember when people used to commit to spending holidays together?"

"It's tough when you're talking three or four generations, though." Jim stayed pragmatic, a good trait in a newspaperman. "Schedules collide. It's not about a lack of commitment. It's about having too many and having to choose between them."

"You're right." Kim's tone echoed her disappointment. "The blessing of Mom's long life means that there are almost two dozen extra people to coordinate with spouses and great-grands. Some of the older great-grandchildren are college age now. That means their schedules don't match anything."

"I know." Janet commiserated as she finished blending Kim's mocha. "Two of Tiffany's friends are coming to our place for Thanksgiving because they can't afford flights to get home and back over the weekend. It's great for us but hard on them, when time and money leave them no choice but to stay at school."

"And that's another part of real life, isn't it?" Jim sampled his sandwich and gave Debbie a thumbs-up. "This is hitting the spot. A simple lunch is something I've learned to appreciate over the years. Sometimes the regular daily stuff means even more than the extraordinary."

"I know I *should* look at it like that," Kim told him. "But I got this idea in my head about having a wonderful Thanksgiving for Mom, and I can't shake it. Christmas is too convoluted for everyone, and viruses have shut down Good Shepherd a few times the last couple of years, so I don't want to assume things will be healthier this winter."

"I hear you. Let me know if I can help in any way," Jim told her. "Not with the cooking, because no one wants that, but if you need trips to airports or depots or bus lines, anything like that, I'll make the time. Sometimes a little help from your friends really pulls things together."

"Thank you."

Janet handed Kim her second coffee. "And you know we're happy to help with whatever you need."

"I know." Kim stood and squared her shoulders. "In my head it was going to work out perfectly. And then this one was busy and that one had commitments elsewhere. I had to bite my tongue not to remind them that this could be their last holiday with Mom, and that made me sad to even think that might be the case. It's not like I can change Mom's timing, especially when we've got so much to be grateful for."

Paulette came over and gave Kim a one-armed hug. "Just go for it," she advised. "Some will come. Some won't. That's just the way of it. Eileen will love whatever you can pull together."

"I agree. That's all you can do," Janet said.

"Sometimes we put a lot of emphasis on those random days we flag on the calendar and forget that the balance of the year is what makes the real difference. Not same old, same old," Paulette continued as she headed for the coffeepot. "Finding joy in the ordinary, like Jim said—that's the stuff a good life is made of."

"You're absolutely right." Kim stood and lifted the two coffees. "I'm going to go ahead with my plans and let the chips fall where they may. If we get half of the relatives here, Mom would be thrilled, and we'd have over twenty-five people."

"That's a nice party in anyone's book." Jim's expression underscored his words. "Better to have twenty-five than not have it at all."

"Yes." Kim gave him a smile of appreciation. "Thank you, guys. I'm sending out a follow-up email as soon as I get home. See you later." She walked out with a lighter step than when she'd come in.

The rest of the day was busy without feeling stressful. Janet finished taking stock of their supplies and submitted her order. By the time they had things washed down and closed up for their Sunday off, she was exhausted. But taking a nap would risk ruining her sleep that night.

She made a strong cup of coffee when she got home and opened her laptop. If Jim and Dani were right about interested developers, there should be something trackable online.

Radner Development, Inc., sprang right up. RDI had purchased over three dozen plots of land throughout Dennison and Uhrichsville in the last five years. It had overseen the building of nearly forty new houses in the area and had recently purchased two multiacre plots of land zoned for residential use.

One of those properties was six minutes from Claymont Creek Farm.

Debbie was with Greg and the boys again that evening. Janet didn't want to disturb their time together, but this was important information. Janet decided to text rather than call, so that Debbie could choose when to respond. THERE'S A DEVELOPER WHO'S BOUGHT LAND NEAR CLAYMONT. LET'S SEE IF HE'S REACHED OUT TO THE ADDISONS ABOUT THE FARM WHEN WE MEET WITH DANI.

GOOD IDEA. ARE YOU RESEARCHING TO STAY AWAKE?

YOU KNOW ME TOO WELL.

Debbie sent back a laughing emoji. HEY, WHATEVER WORKS. SEE WHAT YOU CAN FIND OUT. I'M HELPING WITH EIGHTH-GRADE HISTORY RIGHT NOW. IT'S AMAZING HOW MUCH I DON'T KNOW. GREG'S ON AN EMERGENCY PLUMBING JOB SOMEWHERE IN UHRICHSVILLE, SO JULIAN AND I ARE PLOTTING EXPLORER PATHS IN CENTRAL AMERICA USING TINY PLASTIC BRICKS TO GIVE THE PROJECT A 3D EFFECT.

Janet had done similar projects with Tiffany when she was in middle school. I'LL LEAVE YOU TO IT. SEE YOU TOMORROW.

Then Debbie offered an idea. HEY, THE GUYS ARE GOING BOWLING TOMORROW AFTERNOON. HOW ABOUT WE GET LUNCH AFTER CHURCH THEN HEAD OVER TO THE FARM AND GET AN INSIDER LOOK AT A BUSY WEEKEND?

GREAT IDEA.

Janet printed off the information about Radner Development and tucked it into a folder as Ian came through the door. "Honey, did you realize we've had almost forty new homes built between the two towns in the last few years?" she asked him. "And that Radner Development built almost all of them?"

Ian dished up two bowls of beef stew from the pot Janet had left simmering on the stove. He settled at the table and breathed in the aroma from a fresh loaf of homemade bread. Then he answered, "I wouldn't have known the number Rick had gotten to. I knew it was considerable because the department had to be part of the process." His voice still carried a hint of the brogue from his native Scotland. He pointedly pushed a bowl of stew in front of her.

The department's involvement came as a surprise. "Because?"

"Most of those new homes are on old lots that had to be condemned and cleared. We had to make sure there was no trouble for the demolition crews by absentee landlords or owners of record who'd abandoned properties."

"I've heard of things like that happening," Janet mused, stirring her stew. "I guess I didn't realize how many situations there were. Or that one developer was primarily involved."

Ian sliced bread for her then for himself. "Once the legalities are complete, the demo crew comes in and cleans the lot. Rick had some venture capital and bought a few of the lots at bargain prices. Once that was done, his company built the homes according to the customer's plans with town oversight. The town had to approve the plans so we don't have more eyesores like that uber-modern glass house set between those two classic two-and-a-half stories on the north side. Rick's a good guy. He's got a sharp eye for a solid deal."

"A younger version of Troy Henry?"

Ian acknowledged that with a nod. "Well, yes. But where Troy sticks with commercial investments that pay back long-term,

Rick's into residential. He told me once that his goal is to create neighborhoods for Dennison and Uhrichsville, not just tuck random houses here and there. The town's growing, Janet. Kind of a nice change, right?"

Janet couldn't disagree. "I know my parents were super worried about the population decline twenty years ago. So it's nice to see those abandoned homes fixed up and filled with new families."

He grinned. "New customers, you mean."

She smiled back at him. "That too, and for businesses other than ours. Debbie and I are going to the pumpkin farm tomorrow afternoon while Greg and his boys go bowling."

"Translation: You're snooping under the guise of shopping."

Her guilty look made him grin.

"In case you think of it, I know the gal that supplied their pecan pies." He winked at her. "See if you can snag me one, okay?"

"I sure will, since I totally forgot to leave you one like I usually do. I'm sorry. I was in a sleep-deprived muddle. I'd never forget a treat for my best guy under normal circumstances. But after baking for two days straight?" She yawned. "There's nothing normal about me. There is, however, a pillow with my name on it, and I'm going to go track it down." She gave him a kiss good night. "See you in the morning."

# CHAPTER THREE

*C*laymont Creek Farm was in full swing when Debbie and Janet arrived the following afternoon. Bare-limbed trees had left a carpet of nature's bounty on the ground. The dry weather made the leaves crunch beneath their feet, and two huge "pumpkins" flanked the wide path leading up to the outdoor display area. The pumpkins were actually round hay bales, wrapped in plastic and spray-painted a deep rust-toned orange. A stumpy log stood as the "stem." The big pumpkins offered a warm welcome to the farm.

Beyond the display areas stood the massive converted barn. After housing dairy cows several generations before, the big barn was now a large indoor sales area, filled with the scents and treats of a good harvest.

Janet took in the whole scene. Whitewashed wooden rails ran along the road in both directions. The Addisons had used hundreds of feet of faux autumn leaf garland to dress up the simple farm fencing. Everything about the place invited people to come in, check things out, sample and enjoy. Claymont Creek Farm was a local treasure, and everyone knew it.

Except for whoever was causing problems for the Addison family.

The large red barn stood at the end of the wide path. Tables laden with squash and apples decorated the yard. As the weather grew harsher, those displays would move inside, but for now the yard was full of all things fall.

Dani's parents had added twin wings to the classic red barn decades before. One wing held the cider press and glass-fronted coolers filled with bagged apples. Bins of apples, gourds, ornamental corn, potatoes, and squash framed the other two sides.

The other wing held the bakery, fried cakes, and cider drinks mixed on-site—hot cider, cold cider, and slushed cider in various sizes. Racks of homemade pies, tarts, muffins, and cookies were nestled alongside boxes filled with freshly made cider, chocolate, and fried pumpkin cakes. Some were glazed. Some were dredged in cinnamon sugar. All promised a delicious experience.

The farm embraced the richness of a good harvest, a theme that began with rhubarb in the spring, berries in the summer, and culminated in an explosion of produce when apples, pumpkins, and squash took center stage in autumn.

"This is even busier than I remember." Janet motioned toward the parking lot and the people gathering around the hayrides and the donkey pull. "I haven't been here during the busy season since Tiffany went off to school. We'd come several times a year to pick strawberries and blueberries and also apples. Tiffany loved coming to the farm. It was our tradition."

"As it is for so many other families in the area. I'm amazed at how expansive this is." Debbie scanned their surroundings. "There must be at least a hundred people out here, and the barn is packed."

She was right. Lines had formed at the big bakery counter. There were lines for cider, lines for the fried cakes, and two areas for cashiers. Scents of cinnamon and apple filled the air, and not one person seemed aggravated by having to wait a few minutes for their orders, chattering merrily with those around them.

"Everyone seems so happy," Janet said.

"Why wouldn't they be?" Debbie asked. "They're in their happy place, and no one is doing a money grab over here. That's a huge plus. They get what they pay for. It's a sound business principle."

"Hot cider?" Janet indicated the cider line to their left. "Or hot chocolate?"

"It's a hot chocolate kind of day," Debbie replied. "My treat. How about if you go explore while I wait in line?"

"Glad to." Janet crossed the center of the building. The broad central area of the barn was decked out as an area for families to take fall photos at no charge. There was a large lean-to structure that housed several decorations, such as hay bales, cornstalks, and sheaves of wheat. The frame had displayed and sheltered such decor at the farm for years.

She snapped photos with her phone, grateful for everyone around her who was taking pictures of the beautiful displays, so she didn't seem odd. When she got to the squash and apple wing, the simple beauty of the fall arrangements made her pause.

*God's bounty.*

That was all she could think of as she entered that side. Large bins, baskets, barrels, and shelves were filled with an amazing harvest.

"Hey, Janet!" Dani came her way from an apple display and gave her a quick hug. "Amazing, right?"

"Breathtaking, wholesome, and so busy. Was it always this busy, Dani? I haven't been here in a couple years." She hated to admit that, but it was a simple fact.

"Business has increased by nearly twelve percent each of the last three years." Dani spoke softly, but there was no denying the pride in her voice. "Partially because our towns are growing, but mostly it's social media. It's proven to be the best free advertising there is. People post photos to their pages, others share them, and business just goes up, up, up. I think that's part of what overwhelms Dad."

"I hadn't thought of it that way, how more business would mean more stress at his age." Janet watched as people moved from one display to another, filling bags with various kinds of apples.

"It's so hard to get enough help to make sure things run like clockwork during the farm season but also during the fall. I have a couple of local friends who help by subbing in, but they don't want a seasonal job. Still, they're heaven-sent when they're here because you can see we've got multiple areas that need to be staffed."

"Your dad still does the hayrides?"

Dani nodded. "And Brady oversees the donkey carts on weekends." Brady was the oldest son of Dani's brother, Dean, who ran an auto repair shop in lower Uhrichsville, not far from the depot. "He's at the community college, so it's easy for him to be on hand during the fall weekends. He's good and dependable, like his dad."

"Has he noticed anything odd from his vantage point outside?"

Dani shrugged. "I haven't asked. I probably should have, right? I've stayed quiet because I'm afraid of word getting out or making too big a deal of all this. Dean already thinks it's time for my dad to step down, but they barely talk, so he doesn't say it to Dad. He says it to me. The busyness of fall is great, but it frazzles Dad now that he's in his seventies. And when he's frazzled, Mom's got her hands full to smooth things over. Maybe Dean is right that it's time for them to explore their options."

"He might be." Busy could certainly be hard on some folks. Others, like Dani, thrived on busy. "Or maybe a simple reassignment of tasks? I know your dad is stubborn, so that might be easier said than done. It's not always easy to find a middle ground. But if they do decide to retire, where does that leave you?"

Dani spoke firmly. "I will continue with the farm. I know this business inside out. I can be successful with it. I've been reading this road map all my life." She smiled slightly as she spoke. "I'm an Ecclesiastes 3 kind of gal. You let season follow season. It's a natural path. But now that we've talked about it, I get the feeling that maybe someone doesn't want that to happen. Although I can't imagine who that would be. I know that a developer has been giving out his card to area farmers."

"Would that developer happen to be Rick Radner of RDI?"

"Yes. That's the one. How did you know?"

Before Janet could answer, someone called Dani's name.

She signaled that she would be with them in a second then told Janet in a low voice, "I don't know Rick, but I know he's after land. Well, he can't have mine." She hurried off to a small group of people huddled around the apple display.

Debbie came through the wide opening into the produce wing and handed Janet a steaming travel cup of the Addisons' signature hot chocolate, topped with whipped cream from the dairy farm south of the village.

"Busy place," Janet commented.

"I'll say. The nice weather sure does bring people out. It's got to be hard, though, to have so much of your life dependent on weather,"

Debbie mused. "Late frosts messing with apple blossoms, hailstorms damaging fruit, not enough or too much rain, diseases. Then your fall business depends on having nice weather on weekends. I think I'd be having anxiety issues on a regular basis."

"It's tough when you can't control all the variables," Janet agreed.

"And out west, farmland is being swallowed up by conglomerates and rich people." Debbie swept the barn an appreciative look. "This place shows that bigger isn't always better. With our local population growing, people need someplace to live, and a lot of people want to live outside the hustle and bustle now. They want space, not crowded cities."

"Our little towns are surrounded by lots of beautiful space." Janet headed for the big barn doors, and Debbie fell into step beside her. "But I don't want people to have to drive up to Sugarcreek or Walnut Creek to see pretty farms and stock their pantries. Dani said that Rick Radner's been handing out business cards to the local farmers."

"That's very interesting. Greg's worked with him before. He likes him."

"So does Ian."

"Greg also said that Rick has a shrewd eye for investment." Debbie held the door for Janet to exit then continued to hold it for a cheerful group that bustled inside. Debbie smiled after them then followed her friend. "Apparently, Rick has a keen sense about future trends, and he's done very well with his real estate investments so far. If Rick's trying to add more land for development to his portfolio, it's because he knows the value's going nowhere but up."

They strolled to the wide range of outdoor displays. A sprawling terraced garden separated them from the popular donkey cart track on the other side of the display area. They could see a long line of kids weaving around a large display of pumpkins while adults waited off to the side.

Small bushes and a gorgeous array of mums dotted the space between the displays. The garden tapered as it rounded the near edge of the barn. Fairy houses peeked from between the plants with resin fairies nestled in miniature gardens. The farm offered free scavenger hunts to anyone who wanted to hunt for the fanciful fairies or their homes scattered around the acreage. Currently at least fifteen kids roamed the rock paths woven in and around the garden, searching for items pictured on their laminated sheets.

"It's things like that." Debbie pointed out the kids roaming the garden as they approached. "Affordable things that bring people back every year. And—"

A loud, angry voice by the donkey pull shattered the afternoon peace. "Stop this inhumane practice!" A woman stood on one of the tree trunks that provided natural seating near the area. She unfurled a sign. "Unbridle the donkeys! Let them run free!"

Janet couldn't read the sign from her angle, but the woman's anger and agitation cast a dark cloud on a sun-filled afternoon.

"Stop this practice now! Animals aren't sideshows! They're our friends! Our friends, you hear?"

A Mennonite woman stepped forward. "We use many animals to help us on our farms, *ja*? And they are lovingly cared for."

"Buy a tractor!" The angry woman scoffed at the kindly woman's suggestion. "Strapping horses to plows is as bad as tying donkeys to carts. It's awful! It's inhumane! It should be outlawed!"

"Except it's not, and you're on private property, Hailey." Deputy Brendan Vaughn strode across the upper part of the garden display. The handsome young officer had joined their small force not long after graduating from the police academy.

The woman glared at him. "Someone has to stand up for these poor animals."

"Don't make me cite you," he said, his voice gentle but firm. "I don't want the paperwork, and you don't want another mark on your record. A judge can only deal with so many, and after your last run-in, he warned you to keep on your side of the fencing. *Everyone's* fencing, remember? The judge will have the discretion to raise those fines now. You've been taking up a lot of his time the past few months."

"Because no one wants to hear the truth." She glared at Brendan and folded her arms firmly across her middle. "The donkeys are more important than money. They matter. They matter to me, Officer!"

"Well, they matter to the Addisons and to these nice people trying to have a good time with some wholesome fun," he replied easily. "Because they make money in a very public way for the Addisons, it's in the family's best interests to take good care of them, as you can plainly see. Get off the tree trunk, please. We can talk things over in the parking lot. Or head on home. Leave these people alone, Hailey."

She opened her mouth as if to argue, but then, to Janet's relief, she hopped off the tree stump and stormed toward the parking area.

The deputy followed. "Thanks for your patience, everyone. You can go back to your afternoon now."

Peace should have descended with her departure, but her words clearly bothered some people. Nearly half the customers who had waited in line eased away. Small children cried, wanting their cart ride, and older kids grumbled, but their parents continued to nudge them away from the donkey pull. What had been a pastoral afternoon turned dark, although the sun still shone high in the sky.

Janet and Debbie headed to the parking lot in time to see the woman finish her conversation with Brendan. She angrily made her way to an aging car. She climbed in, slammed the door, and then left.

The two friends approached Brendan.

"Hey, Janet. Debbie." He leaned against his cruiser and folded his arms. "Doing some fall shopping?"

"A farm visit." Janet wasn't going to lie about it, but she didn't have to say more than that either. "This place is absolutely beautiful every fall. About your friend, there." She indicated the road with a slight wave of her hand. "Does she do this kind of thing often?"

The deputy grimaced. "That's Hailey Adams, and unfortunately, she does. Judge Harris keeps warning her, and the fines are starting to get stiff, but she persists. She is a big-time animal lover. She just takes it a step too far sometimes. Like today."

"Is she dangerous?" When Brendan raised an eyebrow, Janet clarified, "I mean, would she do something to physically make a difference? Or does she stick to shouting and making people generally uncomfortable?"

"The latter. So far." Brendan worked his jaw slightly. "Ian and I have talked about this a few times because she seems like she could step up her game, but she hasn't done it yet. She leaves—reluctantly, I'll grant you—when asked and hasn't damaged anything that we're aware of."

"But you feel there's potential?" Debbie asked.

Brendan shrugged. "It's hard to say. There could be, of course. Would she actually do anything to cause harm? We don't think so. But her anger seems to be simmering at a slightly higher temperature lately. That could be cause for concern. I hope I'm wrong," he added as he reached for the car door handle. "I don't want to see her go over the top. But that's up to her, I suppose."

"You handled her well," Janet said.

Brendan laughed. "Ian's taught me a thing or two about keeping the peace. He's a solid role model on how to defuse situations instead of escalating them."

"Should I tell him you said that?" Janet said with a laugh.

"No, ma'am. Can't have it going to the boss's head. There'll be no living with him then."

That made Janet laugh. "True words. Be safe, Brendan."

"Copy that." He got into the cruiser then headed in the direction of the village.

"Interesting turn of events," Janet said to Debbie once they were back in Debbie's car.

"I'll say. She certainly seems angry enough to pull some dirty deals to make things difficult for the Addisons, doesn't she?"

Janet couldn't disagree. "She did indeed. But there's a big step between voicing an opinion and vandalism. Let's make her part of our conversation with Dani on Tuesday, okay? The news has been filled with animal-rights people doing all kinds of things lately, and maybe that kind of reporting has pushed her a little further this fall."

They pulled out of the parking lot with several other cars. Janet had to wonder if they were leaving because the woman's protest had clouded the beautiful afternoon.

# CHAPTER FOUR

When Janet and Debbie approached the Addison barn on Tuesday, Dani was talking with an older man, and she waved them over. "Come meet my neighbor, Mack Jankowski."

The older man smiled and dipped his chin. He was a wiry man of average height. He wore buffalo plaid, a popular choice in the fall, and he seemed downright happy to be talking with neighbors. "Afternoon, ladies. Didn't you use to work down there at the Third Street Bakery?" He posed the question to Janet. "I used to stop by there for your hand pies as often as I could."

"Strawberry rhubarb and lemon," Janet said, recognizing him as well as his usual order. Bittersweet nostalgia touched her heart, but there was no way she could manage a full-scale bakery at the depot site.

Mack grinned. "My two favorites. Saints alive, I miss that place. So many good options, and no matter what day it was, I could walk in there and get pretty much anything I wanted. They don't make places like that anymore."

"We do have a lovely little bakery at the depot," Debbie said.

"And it's a nice place, for sure," Mack agreed. "My friend has come over for your homemade chocolate cream pie every couple of weeks, and I've never had anything better. Every now and again she'll suggest a different kind and I say, 'Mavis, why would we do that when we already know that chocolate cream is the stuff dreams are made of?'"

"That's so nice of you to say. The new place has given me a chance to flex different creative muscles," Janet said. "I didn't realize you missed the hand pies so much. Maybe I'll see if I can get a rotation of them in."

"You call me if you do that. Dani here has my number. Much appreciated. I've got to get on back to my place." He hooked a thumb up the road. "I'm there on the north side of the farm, and I've had the pleasure of being their neighbor for nearly fifty years. I watched Dani and Dean grow up, and I've watched this place thrive."

"That's wonderful," Debbie said.

"Sure is." He patted Dani's arm. "I'll keep my eyes peeled, Dani. I'm glad you told me what's going on. We neighbors have to stick together."

"I appreciate it, Mack."

"Glad to help." He tapped an old and well-worn baseball cap brim with the tip of his finger and headed away toward his own property.

"I decided to fill Mack in while Dad's at the dentist. I figured if we talked out here, no one would overhear the conversation," Dani explained as they made their way to one of the outdoor picnic tables. The weather had held, but there was a cooling trend in the forecast. Already the sun had slid far enough down the horizon to make sweaters a necessity. "Mack's not the worrier that Dad is. But if he's keeping an eye out, he might see something I don't. He won't make something out of nothing, and he won't spread it around."

"I'm glad you have that kind of support," Janet said.

"Me too," Dani said. "His wife passed away a while back, so he's on his own now, and he's got a heart of gold. His kids moved to more populated areas when they finished school, and he's always been kind to me and Dean. And now to Dean's kids. When Kelsey was fighting leukemia nine years ago, Mack ran a fundraising campaign to help Dean and Amelia pay for food and travel expenses. It was six months of treatment in Cincinnati. Amelia was there with Kelsey, and Dean was here with Brady and Ryan. Dean worked night and day to make what money he could, but he traveled back and forth as often as possible. It was a real strain on their time and finances. But Kelsey's doing great now, and that's all that matters, isn't it?"

Janet and Debbie agreed.

Dani straightened on her seat. "Okay, is there anything in particular that you want to pursue?"

Janet and Debbie exchanged glances, and then Janet said, "We met Hailey yesterday."

Dani winced. "Brendan messaged me that he escorted her off the property again."

"Does she come often?" Debbie asked.

"She's pretty regular, yes. The judge has ordered her to stay off our farm, but she comes anyway," Dani said. "We're not her only target either. She pickets the local farmers for all kinds of things that are natural offshoots of an agricultural setting. Milk production, cheese production, meat production—even yogurt production."

"That's like every farm in lower Ohio." Debbie's eyebrows shot up. "Who has time for that?"

"Apparently she does."

"But why?

"I have no idea." Dani frowned. "All I do know is that she targets us and a whole bunch of other places, often at our busiest times because that's when a lot of the things she apparently objects to are happening. She hit Walnut Creek last year during their Journey to Bethlehem because they used sheep and donkeys in their 'stops' along the way to the Nativity. They've also got the big draft horses to pull the wagons of people up to the big barns. She kept screaming at them to get down and walk the first night. I wasn't there, but I heard it created a scene, and nobody wants a scene around a bunch of huge horses and bonfires."

The Journey to Bethlehem was an annual short pilgrimage sponsored by the businesses of Walnut Creek. With its large Mennonite and Amish populations, the little village was able to host thousands of people over their two-day reenactment of Joseph and Mary's trek from Nazareth to Bethlehem. It was a marvelous event that brought the true meaning of Christmas to life in a series of thought-provoking biblical moments. Janet and Ian had taken Tiffany several times over the years.

Janet nudged Debbie. "You and Greg should take the boys this year. They would love it. It culminates at a massive farm filled with all kinds of amazing animals."

"You arrive at the farm on horse-drawn wagons, and they have bonfires going on both sides of the path," Dani added.

"And the Nativity is recreated in the barn with actors, sheep, and a great narrator."

"It sounds marvelous." Debbie made a note on her cell phone then faced Dani. "Has Rick Radner approached you directly about selling?"

"Not me, no. If he's approached Dad, Dad has kept it to himself. But I know he stopped by the Millers' farm and the Ingersons' dairy farm, so he's definitely scouting this area."

"He's got a good eye, then." Janet couldn't fault the guy for that. "Both of those farms have beautiful flat land with a few gentle rolls and great trees. Close to the towns but set off so people can have their own little piece of the pie. Speaking of pie, did they get your oven fixed?"

"Yes, thank goodness." Dani breathed a sigh of relief. "The repairman said it's unusual for an ignitor to go that quickly on a commercial oven, but it's not impossible. So maybe that was simply bad luck?"

"Maybe. But Hailey's arrival, cut fencing, bad gas, clogged pipes, and missing log splitters aren't all bad luck," Janet said. "I think someone's either got a grudge or a plan in mind, and that plan is to make your life difficult."

"So it would seem. Ah, there's Mom and Dad."

The older Addisons parked by the farmhouse. Clint went straight inside, which was highly unusual for such a friendly man.

But Agnes came to the picnic table and greeted all three of them with warm hugs. "It is so good to have you here, Janet and Debbie." She took a step back and looked between the three of them. "Just to have you all together again after all these years. It's marvelous. Dani, we had to make an appointment with the endodontist for Thursday. If they get a cancellation, I'll take your dad in sooner. He's in quite a bit of discomfort, but he'll feel a lot better once that tooth is behaving itself. In the meantime, I'm supposed to keep him on over-the-counter painkillers if I can get him to take them. Sorry he didn't come over to say hello, but I'm sure you understand."

"Of course we do," Janet assured her.

"I also wanted to thank you ladies for stepping in to help us this weekend. It made a big difference. So much of what we do in the fall depends on appearances," Agnes continued. "We want the bins to appear full, the apple coolers stocked, and the bakery up and running at full tilt until Christmas. If people think we're low on things, why come here when they can fill their carts at the supermarket?"

"Because those things aren't nearly as good," Debbie said loyally.

"Thank you for that, and we agree, but you know how people are," Agnes said with a shrug. "Everyone's busy, and no one has the time to run here, there, and everywhere else. For special occasions, yes. But we want people to come here on any old day because our quality sets us apart."

"That's absolutely true," Janet said. "People go out of their way for special occasions and specialty items, but to make it in today's business world, you have to draw in the everyday customer too. You've done that here. Your family has created a strong profile as a weekend attraction while maintaining an everyday shopper experience the rest of the week. I hope Debbie and I have done that at the Whistle Stop too. And great baked goods aren't taken casually."

"I agree." Agnes glanced over her shoulder at the house. "I'm going to get back to your father and make sure he's taken his medicine. Thanks again."

"Our pleasure." Janet waited until Agnes was out of earshot then lowered her voice anyway. "We're going to have a chat with Rick Radner," she told Dani.

"I want to see what kind of neighborhoods he might be pitching in his quest for land," Debbie added.

"In case you need a bigger house?" Dani teased.

Debbie laughed, even as a flush crept into her cheeks. "I'm living in a world ripe with possibilities, it seems," she shot back. "I'm quite open to whatever might occur. I've even discovered a love for football, basketball, and baseball."

"Being a boy mom suits you," Janet quipped, and they all laughed.

"One day at a time, ladies," Debbie reminded them.

Soon, Janet and Debbie said goodbye to Dani and returned to Janet's car.

When Janet turned left onto the main road, Debbie lifted a brow in question. "We never go up this way," Janet explained. "I wanted to get the lay of the land on this side of Claymont Creek Farm. Wow— I'm glad we did."

A beautiful vintage farmhouse appeared on their right. An old wooden sign between thick metal posts read ROSE HILL ORCHARDS. The sign had fruits etched into the four corners of the wooden rectangle, and the distinctive shapes—apple, pear, peach, and plum— were well drawn.

"Is this really an orchard?" Debbie wondered as they slowed down.

"It used to be," Janet replied. "The acreage behind the house used to have peach trees. I remember my dad buying fresh fruit here when I was in elementary school." She pulled off to the side and put her hazards on then rolled down her window. "It's lovely, isn't it? Even without the trees."

"Gorgeous." Debbie sighed softly. "When I was little I dreamed of getting married and living in a big old house like this. It's stunning."

"Ladies, hello!" Mack Jankowski came their way from the opposite side of the road. He motioned to the house with a wave of his hand. "She's a sweet old girl, isn't she?"

"Lovely." Janet indicated the field behind him with a glance. "Do you own both sides of the road, Mack?"

"Sure do. My daddy bought the house and the land before I was a twinkle in his eye. Then when my Rosie and I had been married for three or four years, this side came up for sale and we grabbed it. I inherited this when my parents passed, God rest their souls."

"That was a smart move." Janet said. "They don't make more land, do they?"

"Exactly how we saw it. Rosie's people didn't have much good to say about banks, but I see the good in both. Money in land or in the bank. They always say to diversify your retirement, after all."

"Well, your place is quite pretty." Debbie smiled her appreciation. "It's a joy to behold. And with the curve, you've got a solid vantage point to notice if things are going oddly up the road at Addisons', don't you?"

"You mean that rash of things Dani was talking about?" He frowned. "I can see this and that on occasion, but dark comes pretty quick these days. Anyhow, the one odd thing I've seen lately, besides that lady ballyhooing all over the place about animal rights or whatever it is, is that Charlie Briscoe's truck has gone by and paused now and again."

Charlie Briscoe had been an amazing athlete when Janet and Debbie were in Claymont High. Charlie had gone off to college then made a lot of money in financial markets. He'd been living in Chicago for years.

"Charlie's back in the area?" Janet frowned. "I didn't know that."

"He's one of those so-called gentlemen farmers, I guess." Mack's snort indicated what he thought of that. "They go off to school then come back to the land or some such nonsense. He bought his uncle's place up the road, and you know them college boys."

Debbie offered him a look of confusion. "Meaning?"

Mack removed his hat and scrubbed his hand through his thinning hair. "Know-it-alls. Always chasin' ideas about this, that, and the other thing. You know the type—lots of book learning but barely a lick of common sense. He'll learn like the rest of us, I expect."

"You mentioned seeing his vehicle nearby?" Janet prompted him.

"Yeah. It's a little weird to see his car pulled off up the road, near the donkey pen. From the look of things at his uncle's place, Charlie's running it into the ground. Those who think they know everything often know nothing. I expect he'll sell before things get too bad. His uncle didn't have much to do with us over here, but then Mitchell Briscoe didn't have much of anyone he could call 'friend.' He and Dani's dad had nothing good to say about one another, but I stayed out of that mess."

*Interesting*, Janet thought. She wondered if Dani would be able to shed more light on that situation.

Mack jutted his chin toward Claymont Creek Farm. "The whole thing's got me wondering if Charlie's a chip off the old block. There wasn't a bit of trouble until he bought the Briscoe farm last year." He took a step back from the car. "You ladies have a great day, now. Nice to see you again." He tipped the brim of his faded baseball cap and headed up the driveway.

It made a nice picture, the aged fellow making his way to the classic colonial-style home. The old cedar clapboard wore a fresh coat of white paint, and the shutters featured a faded rose tone that perfectly set off the olive-green window boxes and door.

"That place truly is gorgeous." Debbie tapped some information into her phone. "It has about fifty acres going back to Claymont Creek Farm, and frontage on both roads. Stunning. It's valued at a cool half million."

Janet whistled. "Whoa. A nice retirement indeed."

"Land always boosts the price," Debbie said. "But what a pretty house. The yard, the setting—it's so idyllic."

"It is one of the prettiest old farmhouses I've seen, and he sure keeps it up nicely. The old-fashioned landscaping and the offset garage complete the image, don't they?"

"Like those Currier and Ives farmhouse prints my mom collects."

Janet and Ian had pledged not to delve into Debbie's relationship with Greg Connor, but Janet didn't miss the wistful note in Debbie's voice as she studied the inviting home.

Debbie had been denied her hoped-for future once when her fiancé died overseas twenty years before, but as weeks went by, there was no doubt that Janet's wonderful friend was falling for Greg. He seemed to be falling just as hard, but falling in love was different with kids involved. There were more than two hearts in this equation. There were four. That was an important factor for Debbie and Greg.

But as Janet watched Debbie dreaming over the old farmhouse, she sent a prayer heavenward that her dear friend's wishes would come true soon.

# CHAPTER FIVE

*K*im popped into the café at the same time as early morning regular Harry Franklin the next day.

Harry visited them nearly every day from his home around the corner. The house gave him a full view of the depot and the museum from his back windows, and Harry was quick to let folks know that it was a view he cherished. Harry had worked at the depot during World War II then stayed on to be a train conductor for decades afterward. At ninety-six, Harry was sound of mind and limb. He was a big fan and staunch supporter of both the café and the depot museum. His dog, Crosby, trotted at his side with his usual canine joy.

"Good morning, Kim." Harry flashed a bright smile Kim's way. "We've got the chill in the morning air now, don't we?"

"Sure do. Most of the leaves are gone, but I don't mind this gentle patch of weather one bit," Kim replied. "I'll take it for as long as the Good Lord offers it, because we all know what's coming."

"Old man winter, sure enough." Harry slid onto a stool at the counter before greeting Janet and Debbie. "Good morning, ladies. You're mighty festive this morning."

Janet showed off her long-sleeved version of a fall T-shirt with the famous quote, A PARTY WITHOUT CAKE IS JUST A MEETING. "Gotta love fall, my friend. What can we get you this morning? Eggs over easy?"

Harry mulled it over then shook his head. "I'm in a scrambled-eggs mood. With rye toast, please."

"And the same for our friend Crosby?" Debbie asked.

"Except without the toast for him," Harry said, holding up a finger. "The veterinarian says we need to get Crosby's weight down. She says it's the best thing for him, and I want him to be around for a good long time yet."

"No problem. I'll have this out in a few." Debbie ducked into the kitchen.

Janet set about getting coffees for Harry and Kim.

Harry tapped the counter. "So, Kim, what's the deal with that old box you've got?"

"It contains a mystery that I'm hoping to get some help with." Kim set an antique-looking box between them on the counter. The box was covered or wrapped in some kind of tea-stained floral satin, giving it a unique vintage appearance. "Abby Meyers found this in the back of a closet. She was cleaning out one of her uncle Red's rentals for Greg to get it ready to rent or sell. They're not sure which way they want to go yet. Anyway, Abby brought this around to me because it had World War II medals and pins and bars inside, as well as this pack of letters." She opened the box and withdrew a thin bundle tied with a pale green ribbon.

"Are these letters from the front?" Janet asked as she studied the envelopes. "There's a piece of history here. Can we send them to the family if they've moved on? Or drop them off if they're still local?"

"We could, except all the identifying information has been redacted."

Janet drew back, surprised. "Who redacts personal mail? And after it's been delivered?"

"My questions exactly," Kim replied, taking a sip of coffee.

With Kim's permission, Janet untied the bundle of letters for closer examination. On each envelope, the addressee's name and address were blacked out, as was the return address. There was a sheen to the ink used, and the blacked-out areas were applied with precision, as if the person needed the redactions to be neat and complete. "This is weird."

"Isn't it?" Kim asked. "Why would someone want personal letters to remain a mystery?"

Debbie emerged from the kitchen with Harry's breakfast order. She seemed to have overheard Kim's question. "The postmarks should give us a clue, right?" She made a face as she looked more closely at the envelopes. "Never mind. The postmarks are blurred. Anything else you'd like right now, Harry?"

"Not a thing." He inhaled the aroma of the freshly cooked eggs Debbie set before him. "Thank you kindly, Debbie. From me and Crosby here."

"I'll give Crosby his breakfast once it's cooled off." Debbie made sure Harry's mug was filled before turning back to Kim and Janet. "Kim, you said Red owned the rental?"

"He did, but it was rented out for more than five decades. It looks like every identifying mark has been gone over on these love letters—"

"Love letters?" Janet opened the top one and carefully withdrew the single folded page from within. "'My dearest wife,'" she read. "'I have counted the days since I left you, and I'm counting the ones until I see you again. Our short time together did nothing but make me long for you more. I love you, darling, and I kiss your picture each morning and each night. The thought of you, my precious wife, is what keeps me going.'" Janet clasped the letter to her chest. "Oh my goodness. I don't know if I can bear the thought of what happened to her and him."

"Every letter is like that," Kim said. "There are six of them. None too long, but that's probably normal, because I don't think guys had a lot of time to write during daylight hours. None of the letters contain a single clue about who wrote it or where he was writing from, though I'm guessing from the handwriting that the same person wrote all of them. He was clearly anxious to come home."

"And each one begins the same way, with 'my dearest wife'?" Janet guessed.

"That's right. But we don't know who that wife is or was, and we don't know why anyone would leave a precious bundle like this in the closet. Was it overlooked? Or deliberately left? I'd dig into it myself, but with the Christmas Train season, Thanksgiving plans, visiting with Mom, and redecorating the whole place for the holidays, I don't have time. I know you gals are busy too, but you're better than I am at solving mysteries. I keep thinking what a nice gift this would be for someone who might have a connection to these letters, and how wonderful it would be to get them before Christmas, but I know I can't do it justice."

Janet exchanged a glance with Debbie. "We might not be able to do any better, but we'll give it a try."

Debbie lifted one of the letters and examined the envelope. "Airmail stamp and the old postmark they used for military mail. There must have been some water damage at some point, because the postmarks and stamps are smeared."

"There's an interesting precision to the blacked-out sections, and the careful way each letter is folded on its original crease," Janet added. "Can we find out who lived in the house? Which property was it, Kim?"

"The one on East Sixth Street in Uhrichsville."

"That's close to where I worked at the Third Street Bakery." Janet tapped the letter with her pointer finger. "Nearly everyone in that neighborhood came into the bakery at one time or another, especially at holiday time. And there are a few who've lived in that neighborhood for decades. Maybe one of them could shed some light on this."

"You don't mind?" Kim finished her coffee and stood. "I've got to get some work done. We have a school field trip scheduled at nine thirty. I need to be prepared for that and get a handle on those Christmas decorations for each railcar."

"We'll take care of it, Kim," Janet assured her.

"Thank you so much." Kim hurried out. Kim hurried everywhere this time of year. The Christmas Train rides were a big draw for both the depot and the café, and Kim had the responsibility to dot all the i's and cross all the t's, as hundreds of people would stream in and out of the depot over the late November and early December weekends.

Debbie held up one of the letters. "We're going over that way tomorrow to chat with Rick Radner, right?"

"He said we could stop by between two and three. His office is dead center between the old bakery, Red's rental house, and a couple of the locals I got to know over the years. I'll call them a little later in the day." Janet picked up Kim's mug. "Maybe we can see them too."

"Yes, let's." Debbie tucked the letter back into the folds of the ribbon. "I love the sentiment these offer. But that redacting is weird, Janet. As if someone wanted to make sure no one knew where these letters went. Or where they were from. Why redact both addresses so fully?"

"An illicit correspondence?" Janet suggested.

"To 'my dearest wife'?" Debbie asked.

"Maybe he didn't survive the war, and his widow remarried and didn't want the second husband to know she kept the letters? Or the person in the rental kept them for someone else?"

"I hadn't thought of that. The only reason I can think of to redact both the return address and the addressee is to keep anyone from knowing about the romance. Right?"

"Or life intervened and everything that could go wrong, did," Janet replied.

Harry swallowed a bite of rye toast. "That's not World War stuff, girls. The medals were, sure. But those letters weren't written in the forties."

Janet sent him a puzzled look. "How do you know?"

"I've seen a lot of wartime letters. That specific stamp came out toward the end of the Vietnam War. Once a person was deployed, postage was free, so maybe the first two were from boot camp and the others from overseas. Another thing is there's always a number in the return address." He tapped the redacted upper corner. "That's a code that tells where the soldier was stationed. Sometimes it resembles a zip code, but not always. The box these were stored in is newer, but that doesn't say much, because I recall my missus having a couple of those over time. Fancy paper came in them. With envelopes too."

"Stationery boxes." Debbie began to wipe down the counter. "That's why it was familiar. I had a couple in high school. They looked vintage, and I loved them."

Harry smiled. "Sylvia did too. Once the paper was used up, she hung on to those boxes. She put keepsakes and such in them. They're not worth a lot of money, but a lot of good memories were preserved in ours."

"So, more recent than we've been thinking." Janet gave Harry a quick hug. "That's a huge help, Harry."

He ducked his head, blushing a little. "Well, my memory's not perfect, but it's not all that bad either. Glad to help."

Janet stored the box beneath the counter, out of sight. If Harry was right, whoever had rented Red's house might have been the owner of the letters. It was a long shot. But if the letters were from more recent times, the odds of them finding the original owner were much higher than she'd thought.

## CHAPTER SIX

T here's RDI." Janet pointed, and Debbie flicked on her signal to make the turn into the double-wide driveway.

She gave the older home a quick once-over as her friend parked. The one-and-a-half story house was done in a Craftsman bungalow style. The inviting porch was finished with stone-based pillars, and the cedar siding was painted a deep forest green, trimmed in ivory. The home was well preserved. As they climbed the five broad front steps, the deep porch offered a welcome reprieve from the afternoon shower that had begun during the short drive.

"Great house, isn't it?" Janet asked. "It's got lines like yours."

"Substantial but cozy," Debbie agreed.

The door opened before they had a chance to ring the bell. A medium-height man dressed in business casual gave them a frank, easygoing smile. "Ladies, come on in. I saw Ian yesterday," he added, standing back to usher them inside. "He and Greg were checking out some damage from an accident near the medical complex, and I was caught in the traffic."

"He was happy that no one was seriously hurt," Janet replied. "He told me how you've renovated a substantial number of houses in Dennison and Uhrichsville over the last five years or so. That's impressive. I took a quick drive and saw several of them. You did a really nice job."

"Greg worked on at least half of those properties," Rick replied. "I hire him whenever he's available, but the praise is appreciated."

He led them into an office that held two desks and a large round table. Twin bookshelves flanked an updated fireplace, a favored Craftsman touch. Lead-paned windows were set over each bookshelf. The old-fashioned windows allowed late-day light into the room, although the rain had darkened the skies considerably.

The table offered room for eight people to sit. Janet took a seat, Debbie chose the one to Janet's right, and Rick took one opposite them, allowing them room and solid eye contact. "So how can I help you ladies today?"

"Development plans." Janet spoke frankly, assuming Rick would be honest with them unless he had something to hide. "We have friends with farmland outside of Dennison, and they're worried that you're trying to buy up a considerable share of farmland and develop it into a suburban-style housing neighborhood."

"And they're absolutely correct."

Janet blinked in surprise. Well, she had wanted honesty, and that was what she got.

Debbie pointed to a graphic mounted on the wall opposite the bigger desk. "Is that a schematic for your proposal?" When Rick nodded, she got up and crossed the room. After studying it for a moment, she observed, "This isn't the Addison farm area."

He stood and crossed to her side at the schematic, Janet on his heels. "No, this is closer to town. People like the proximity to the amenities the towns offer, but a lot of buyers are looking for a house with some land. I'm proposing two-acre lots for this neighborhood. That way people aren't on top of one another. They'll have room for a yard, a garden, a pool, even a good-size shed, but they'll still be conveniently located near town."

"That does sound nice," Janet said.

"We hope so. But why would any developer want to ruin a jewel like Claymont Creek Farm?" He sounded genuinely bewildered by the idea. "Places like that and the Dennison Depot, plus our proximity to tourist places like Sugarcreek and Walnut Creek are a huge draw to our area now. With the promise of new job opportunities—"

"What opportunities?" Debbie interrupted.

"A new metal fabricating plant is being proposed for the industrial site between here and New Philadelphia," he explained. "They're revitalizing an old plant to conform to the new standards. When that was approved, a major tech investor decided that putting a tech complex there would be smart. Between the two, we'll be getting around fifteen hundred good-paying jobs. That's a lot of new income coming into the area."

Debbie and Janet exchanged looks. "So you're not targeting the Addison farmland?" Janet clarified.

Rick shook his head. "Nothing like that has ever crossed my mind. Like I said, people love the idea of farm-to-table production, and a thriving farm like the Addisons' is more useful as an attraction. It adds to the small-town, homey feel that helps persuade people to move into my other properties. Developing it would actually hurt my current venture."

Janet never would have guessed that.

"However, I'm not the only person expanding my new housing opportunities," he mused, almost as if to himself. "I don't have names right now, but there are two developers from the New Philadelphia area who are interested in similar projects now that the industrial approvals have gone through. If you have any influence with the Addison family, I'd advise them not to sell. If they'd like to talk to me about why I'm saying that, I'm more than happy to sit down with them. They're the kind of business every developer wants to have within minutes of their neighborhoods, and I don't think it would be in their best interest to sell either."

"Thank you for being transparent with us," Janet said. "We were afraid that the Addison land was being targeted surreptitiously, and we're grateful for your honesty."

"Transparency is crucial to my business," Rick said. "What goes around comes around. Honesty and integrity have kept me on the right path since I started this business sixteen years ago. My grandparents raised me when my parents decided that being parents cramped their style, and I'm forever in their debt. They were salt of the earth and taught me to live my life according to Scripture in every aspect. They left me this house when they passed away. Owning this place taught me a lot about keeping up property values, efficiency, and solid construction. These old Craftsman houses have great bones. Their bequest went way further than giving me a home. It gave me a business for life."

"They sound like wonderful people." Janet scanned the home's interior. "And you're right. This place has everything anyone could want, with the built-ins and all." She indicated the bookshelves and the pocket door separating the office from an oak-trimmed dining area. "These nooks and crannies give older homes such character. Rick, thanks for meeting with us." She extended her hand. "And best of luck with all you do."

"My pleasure, ladies." He shook their hands then let them out.

The rain was heavier now, and they dashed to the car.

Once in, Janet faced Debbie. "I believe him."

"No reason not to with the proof on the wall," Debbie said. "Perhaps it's the developers from New Philadelphia making things difficult for the Addisons. Maybe they're trying to make it too hard for Dani to take over."

Janet weighed that briefly. "But his point makes sense. Wouldn't the other developers feel the same way? That local attractions draw in visitors?"

"I think that depends on the developer," Debbie said. "Plus, developers from other towns might not realize what a boon the farm is to our local economy."

Janet supposed that was possible.

"And Rick is a straight shooter, but that doesn't mean the other developers follow the same MO," Debbie continued. "But I'm still leaning toward Hailey as our troublemaker. After all, we've seen her in action."

"We sure have. She wasn't afraid to make her point in broad daylight, surrounded by witnesses."

Debbie started the car, put it into gear, and carefully backed out of Rick's driveway. "Were you able to get ahold of some of your customers from the bakery?"

"Lori Rosen is up on North Dawson. Her sister-in-law, Doris Tewksbury, is on Sixth Street, but she's going to meet us at Lori's place. Lori asked if we could bring some treats, so I've got a little box of peanut butter fudge whoopie pies in my tote bag."

"Bribing people, are we?" Debbie asked with a smile.

Janet smiled back. "I prefer the term 'coaxing.' Nothing like one great memory to spur another. Both Lori and Doris loved our fudge-filled sandwich cookies at the Third Street Bakery."

"Peanut butter and chocolate is always a winning combo." Debbie parked in a lot where Janet directed. The women exited the car and walked two doors down to Lori Rosen's home.

The elderly woman met them at the door. Janet was pretty sure she'd been waiting and watching, and the twinkle in her blue eyes showed her excitement at their arrival. "How wonderful to see you again, Janet. Please come in."

She stepped back to allow them inside, and Janet hugged her. "It's great to see you too, Lori."

Their hostess led them into a classic, cozy kitchen. "The rain's let up some, hasn't it? I was worried that you might have to park farther up the road and get drenched, but it's worked out just fine."

Doris Tewksbury started to get up from the kitchen table, but Janet spotted her wince of pain and waved her back into her seat. "I can give you a hug without you moving a bit, Mrs. Tewksbury." She reached down and gave the woman a gentle embrace. "You and your kindnesses were well-known all the while I worked on Third Street. That hug's a long overdue thank-you for all you did for others."

"Mercy, I miss that bakery now that I don't drive so well." She shrugged and sighed. "Getting on in years isn't for sissies, let me tell you."

Janet slid into the seat on the adjacent side of the table. "I would be happy to drop things off to you. I do it for several of my previous customers who can't walk to find me anymore. I'm over this way on a regular basis." She slid a card across the table. "You call and put in an order anytime, and I'll make sure it gets to you. Okay?"

"You wouldn't mind?" Surprise lifted her brows and brightened her demeanor. "I'd be much obliged. Thank you, Janet."

"Happy to do it," Janet assured her as Debbie took the seat opposite the two older women. Janet set the box of cookies on the table. "I've brought a treat, and we've come to pick your brains about something that may have happened a long time ago. By the way, this is my friend and business partner, Debbie Albright."

"It's lovely to meet you, Debbie," Lori said. "As for picking our brains, old things I can remember. Yesterday is another story altogether. Current times seem to get lost in a bit of a fog these days."

"Then old is good." Janet winked at her then pulled out a map of the area she'd printed off the night before. "Red Meyers owned a few properties around here."

"And he was a decent landlord too," Doris said. "That makes all the difference, you know. That's why people didn't hop, skip, and jump from place to place a few decades ago. A good landlord is a valuable thing to have."

"It sure is." Janet tapped her finger on a house she'd circled. "What can you tell me about this one?"

"Next to Myrt Donnell's place. Myrt owned this one alongside. And the Browns lived hereabouts." She pointed across the street from Red Meyers's rental. "Selma and Landon. He passed on, and they sold the place about thirty years back. Saints alive, that sounds so long. Then I realize it was the nineties and not so long ago at all."

"There's a lot of truth in that," Lori said. "Weren't the Murphys right next door to the Browns?"

"Two doors down. The Dubonnet family had that house between them for a decade or better. It was the Karras family before them and then again after, which was no coincidence." Doris pointed at another house near Red's well-kept duplex.

"How did that come about?" Debbie asked.

"A granddaughter wanted to buy her grandma's house, so she did. They're still there. The Brinkmans. Nice family, two kids in college now. That woman understands the value of family and heritage. Her grandma, Letitia Karras, moved in with them a few months back. Lettie lived crosswise from Red's place a good long while. She'd be a good person to talk to. And over there, in Red's rental?" Doris frowned. "I don't recall specifics. I'm sorry. What about you, Lori?"

"I didn't walk up that way very often," Lori admitted. "But I don't remember a bit of trouble with anyone on either side of the street. Is that what you're after, Janet? A troublemaker?"

"No," Janet said. "Red's niece found some old letters there. We want to direct them to the right person. Nothing too sinister."

"Fixing the little things from a broken past sometimes puts people back together. But sometimes it makes them go asunder," Doris said. "I'm always careful to tread lightly on someone's past."

Where Doris stayed firmly in her practical nature, Lori tended to wax poetic. "There might be tender hearts tucked within yesterday's words. Old times are good for some and rough for others. One rarely knows what will help and what will hurt these days."

Janet exchanged a glance with Debbie. They'd seen that for themselves a few times since starting their business. "We'll tread lightly, Lori. I promise."

"I know you will." Lori opened the box of cookies. "You remembered my favorite." She beamed as she set the chocolate-stuffed whoopie pies on a small ceramic plate.

When Janet and Debbie finally returned to the car, the rain had picked up again. Janet's phone chimed a reminder. "I have to get home. We're doing a sandwich supper tonight because Ian's addressing a school meeting about the dangers of kids and social media."

Debbie groaned as she started the car. "How does a parent ever get that right these days? Kids and phones, putting the entire internet into their inexperienced hands and hoping it turns out all right."

Janet and Ian had put limits on Tiffany's phone and social media use when she was younger, but they both knew how easy it was for kids to get around those limits if they wanted to. If one kid didn't know how, the next kid did. Then they'd share it on social media. "You can set all the rules you want, but if parents don't follow through and check up on things, the rules are easily broken. We figured the best way to combat all of that was to wait and not let Tiffany have a phone until she was fifteen."

"Prudent."

"We thought so. But we also made sure she understood the dangers that lurk out there, as well as the positives. With Ian being a cop, he was great at explaining the realities to her. But then you send them off to college or a job, and you pray."

"Greg says that the youth group has been a great outlet for the boys' excess energies. That and their busy sports schedules. He says if you keep them too busy to get into trouble, it's much harder for them to find trouble."

"And that's the truth of the situation. It's never easy, but it's always worth it." Janet straightened in her seat and got back to business. "I'll try to contact the Karras family and set up a time to see them."

"And I'm going to do a deep dive into those developers from New Philadelphia." Debbie pulled into Janet's driveway and put the car into park. "I think Rick is telling the truth, but another developer might not operate the way he does, so they might be harassing Dani's family and their farm. People stir up trouble to keep a lid on prices."

"You're right." Janet reached for the door handle. "Let me know if you find anything of interest."

"I could do my research here," Debbie offered. "I'll stop at home to eat then come back after Ian's gone to the meeting."

Janet bit her tongue. She'd hoped to make some significant progress on the cookbook project she'd been working on. The finished work would be a gift to Debbie, a surprise for a dear friend who'd opened a door for Janet at just the right time. Debbie had taken a leap of faith by coming back to Dennison after a lucrative career in Cleveland. Her idea to open the café came as the owner of Third Street Bakery had retired, spelling the end of Janet's job in Uhrichsville.

But if Debbie wanted to work together this evening, Janet would squeeze time out of another day to make progress on *Whistle Stop Recipes*, a fun collection of Dennison history and bestselling recipes. "Or you could stay and have supper with us. Then we can dig in."

Debbie's phone chimed. She scanned the screen and visibly brightened. "Well, not to insult you or your amazing sandwich supper, but I just got an offer of homemade red sauce and meatballs over rigatoni. It seems Greg finished up that emergency call a little early. But I'll still delve into possible developers once I'm back home."

"Then I'll see you in the morning." Janet exchanged a knowing look with Debbie. "Never let it be said that I interfere in affairs of the heart. Especially when I'm so happy for you. Rigatoni sounds wonderful with all this rain. Catch you later." She hurried from the car to the house.

Once Ian had left for the parents' informational meeting, she jumped into the cookbook project and managed to typeset the cookie section to her satisfaction. The project was coming along. Debbie would love it. Maybe they would offer the cookbook for sale in the café.

She'd been snapping pictures for months, and she'd actually had to measure some recipes she'd created in a more slapdash manner. The phrases "a little of this" and "a splash of that" didn't translate well in cookbook terms. Many home bakers needed more exact instructions than "until it feels right."

But Janet needed confirmation that her instructions worked across the board, so she called Dani. "Can you whip up a couple of recipes I'm developing to make sure they read sensibly and the instructions are clear?"

"It would be my pleasure." Dani sounded more upbeat than she had last week. It was a refreshing change, especially during the farm's busy holiday season. "How about if you email them to me? I might be able to get to them sometime tomorrow."

"That would be great. Thank you."

Janet checked her watch. Time for one last thing before bed. She entered the Karras name into the search bar, and it didn't take long to find a phone number for them. Their proximity to Red's rental property might not yield anything of note, but she and Debbie had discovered that one thread often led to another when researching. Lettie and her family might not know anything about the people who'd lived in Red's place forty years before, but they might know someone who did. That could make all the difference.

# CHAPTER SEVEN

*J*anet buzzed into the Addisons' sales barn a little after three the following afternoon. The rain had let up around midday, but the dank, cool air still lingered. The wind had picked up too, and there were no happy shoppers wandering the thinning outdoor displays.

The interior of the barn made a very different impression. Scented pine cones filled the air with the fragrance of cinnamon as Janet stepped inside. The warm smell inspired thoughts of toasty fires, family gatherings, and holiday meals. The outside squash tables were being downsized because of the colder weather, but the Addison crew had heaped up their inside displays with all things fall.

The far wall had been lined with bins of apples when Janet was a girl. Now efficient coolers were stocked with bags of gorgeous varieties. The cider area was well stocked, and a neighboring farm's homemade eggnog had been added since Janet's last visit. She grabbed two quarts of it and went in search of Dani.

She approached the clerk at the bakery counter. "Is Dani here?"

"She sure is. She's through there." The woman nodded toward the swinging door leading to the kitchen. The fried cakes for which they were known were made out here, in full view of the customers, but the big ovens were in the bakery kitchen.

Janet started to the door but stopped when she heard the low rumble of unhappy voices from the kitchen.

She hesitated, not wanting to interrupt a private exchange. She stepped aside and texted Dani instead. HEY, I'M HERE. SHOULD I COME TO THE KITCHEN?

The voices paused. Short seconds later Dani's brother charged through the door. Dean didn't slam it, probably because swinging doors don't slam, but he appeared angry enough to slam something. He stormed across the barn and went outside.

Dani emerged from the kitchen after him, frowning. When she saw Janet, she folded her arms over her chest. "Family drama. Sorry."

"Happens to all of us," Janet assured her. "Is Dean all right?"

"He's stressed. His mechanic business is doing well, and he's good at what he does, but Dad keeps calling on him to fix this or that. Dean interrupts his work, takes the time to do triage and order parts, and then gets the work done. He doesn't expect Dad to pay him for his time, but he really does need him to pay for the parts. He has a family to care for, after all. It's been going on for a long time, but Dean hates to say anything because Mom and Dad helped them out when Kelsey was sick."

Dani moved into the kitchen, and Janet followed her. "That sounds potentially tricky to navigate."

"I know Dad gave Dean and Amelia a significant amount of money when Kelsey was fighting leukemia. They had to take a lot of time off work. Amelia stayed with Kelsey in Cincinnati, and Dean traveled back and forth often to see them. Of course, that costs money, and he couldn't take side jobs on weekends because he was with Amelia and Kelsey."

"As he should have been," Janet said.

"Brady and Ryan stayed here at the farm so that Dean was free to work," she continued. "St. Jude directed Kelsey's treatment but let them be closer to home by using the Cincinnati hospital. Once she was better and they were back home, Dad tried to pay Dean for the repairs he'd done, but he wouldn't take it."

"Understandable. Your family's like mine—we like to help one another."

"Right, but since then Dean has done more repairs and feels like he's being taken advantage of. He wants Dad to pay for the parts." Dani rolled her eyes. "But, being men, neither one will broach the subject with the other. Dean feels guilty about being upset, and Dad's placidly going along as if it's okay. He probably has no idea Dean feels any kind of way about it because they talked about it once."

"Can you bring it up to your dad?" Janet asked.

"I did this past year, but Dad kind of shrugged it off as if I was worrying about things I shouldn't, that he was still able to run the finances around this place even if he forgets a thing or two now and again. I think he's forgotten all about it since then." She made a face. "Stubborn men, both of them."

"How does Dean feel about your parents selling the farm?"

"He's fine with the idea," Dani admitted. "He doesn't think I can handle running the whole thing by myself, and I think he's right. But I can certainly hire people to help with planting and harvest, like Dad does. You can't work in a business like this for over twenty years and not know how to put a crew together, how to work until dark and after, and how to keep things updated so you don't get kicked in the head with a huge bill all at once. Mom and Dad have been training me on every area for years, so I think I'm the ideal person to take on this operation."

"The size doesn't scare you?" Janet had plunged into a new business the previous year, but she had a partner. Having backup was huge, and she suspected the café's operation was much smaller than the farm's.

Dani opened her mouth then closed it, as if reconsidering. When she answered, her reply felt rehearsed. Maybe she had to repeat herself to family every time the question came up. "I've got knowledge and faith on my side. And I wouldn't be completely alone. There are plenty of seasonal workers that help even if it gets sporadic. I'd work it out with Dean to buy his share. The farm makes money. Even in a bad year, we generally come out okay."

"But that's because it's paid for, isn't it?" Janet had looked into setting up her own bakery when the Uhrichsville bakery was closing, but the amount of investment and overhead had made it prohibitive. Going into it with Debbie as a smaller business had been the perfect solution.

"Yes and no. Our family owns the farm, but I would have to buy Dean out," Dani said. "Dean sees Dad's worries growing. He sees him as a tired, aging man, and he thinks that if developers are knocking at the door with significant offers, it's selfish on my part not to take them. That's what we were arguing about. Dean thinks I'm putting their retirement at risk, and I believe I'm saving a family tradition, a three-generation farm that's on solid ground."

Janet hesitated to voice her next question, but decided asking was better than wondering. "Could Dean be behind the weird things happening? Is he angry enough to take matters into his own hands?"

Dani hesitated, indicating that Janet wasn't alone in her concern, but then Dani shook her head. "No. He wouldn't do that. At least I don't think he would, but his agitation is growing."

"There could be another reason for that, though," Janet pointed out. "He sees a thriving business, bringing in a solid income, yet no one's paying him for his work. That's the scenario from Dean's point of view, isn't it?"

Dani blinked in surprise. "I guess I hadn't thought of it that way. He does kind of stay away during the fall. Amelia brings Kelsey and Ryan over to help out on the busy weekends. Brady works here on the weekends, running the donkey cart exhibit. Ryan just turned fifteen. He said he wants to start working here all through the summer next year. Dean hasn't been what you'd call supportive of that idea," she admitted. "He suggested that Ryan find a job at a pizza shop or the grocery store. Something with 'staying power.'"

Janet winced.

"Even with that, I don't think Dean would deliberately undermine us. We're family. He has some strong opinions about me buying the farm, but he'd never do anything to harm the farm."

Janet wasn't so sure. Nothing major had been done so far. The vandalism hadn't been dangerous or life-threatening. It was merely a constant bother, the kind of thing someone might do if they wanted to tip the scales in their favor.

She put a hand on Dani's shoulder. "You know your brother better than I do. Debbie and I are looking into Hailey Adams, of course, as well as a couple of developers who are scoping properties in this area. On top of that, we ran into Mack the other day, and he told us he's seen Charlie Briscoe's truck pulling off the road not far from here a time or two."

Dani's eyes went wide. "Mack said that?"

"Yes, and he mentioned that there was bad blood between your dad and Mitchell Briscoe, Charlie's uncle. I was surprised to hear that Charlie had come back to town after doing so well in business and finance."

"You're right." Dani gave her a nervous smile. "Dad and Mitchell Briscoe disagreed on everything, and that stubbornness set in. Dad loves his family, but he's not good about giving others second chances. He was unkind to Mitchell, Mitchell responded in kind, and they both ordered one another to stay off their properties. Land wars. It was ridiculous. You know?"

"Agreed." Janet's phone chimed with a calendar reminder.

Dani stepped back. "You need to see how your recipes came out, and here I am, going on and on about family stuff. Sorry, Janet. Come on back." She led Janet into the kitchen.

"No apologies needed. We all need to vent in a safe place now and then," Janet assured her. "And hey, those Danish look marvelous, don't they?"

Dani agreed. She seemed much more at ease talking about baked goods than the current farm problems. "They came out perfect, and I followed the timing and the recipe exactly. Same with the apple pie tarts. I did the second batch with a slightly thinner crust because the first ones seemed disproportionate, but I think that was my fault rather than the recipe's."

"Good to know. I can add crust thickness to the recipe to help others avoid that issue." Janet made a couple of notes in her phone then gave Dani a quick hug. "I have to get going, but you hang in there. We'll figure this out, so try not to worry. Thank you so much for running through those recipes for me. It's a huge help."

"Glad to do it." Dani returned the hug. "And thank you for checking things out quietly. I felt like I was alone in this until you and Debbie offered to help last week. That wasn't a nice feeling."

"I'm sure it wasn't. But it also shows your kind and caring heart, watching out for your mom and dad like that."

Janet called Debbie on her way home and filled her in on Dean's long-standing issue with his father. "It's amazing how something like that wears on people," she mused while Debbie murmured agreement. "A simple conversation might clear the air, but he's reluctant to confront his father, who sounds like he's kind of clueless about the whole thing."

"It's so frustrating when you're on the outside and can see a problem threatening a relationship, and you can also see a simple solution, but you can't implement it for the people involved," Debbie said.

"So frustrating," Janet agreed. "I care about Dani and therefore her family, so I want to fix this for them. But I can't."

"They're a strong family," Debbie assured her. "They'll work it out." She paused then added, "As long as Dean isn't the one behind the sabotage out at the farm. Goodness, do you think that's a possibility?"

"I can't decide," Janet admitted. "Dani claimed not to think so, but she seemed almost hesitant to make that claim. But maybe I was reading into it when she was simply making sure she thought the idea all the way through. I don't want to believe it was Dean, but we may have to explore that option if our others don't pan out."

"I hope one of them does. Not that I want someone to be sabotaging the farm at all, but since that's clearly happening, I hope that a member of the family isn't behind it." Debbie sucked in a breath. "Is that the time? Sorry, I have to go pick up Jaxon from basketball practice. I'll see you in the morning."

"See you." Janet hung up as her house came into view.

A strange vehicle was backed into her usual spot in the driveway, a dark SUV with the engine running.

Before she reached the driveway and could see who it was, the SUV pulled out and drove away. Perhaps it had simply been someone who'd pulled over to get directions on their phone.

She had just parked when she saw Ian parking in the driveway behind her.

He got out of his car and met her as she got out of hers. "Did you know who that was?" he asked.

"I didn't recognize the car," she said.

Ian grinned as he held the door for her to step into the house. "You're sure no one was coming to see you about the café? Or the cookbook? Or maybe you and Debbie have stirred the pot by checking things out for Dani Addison."

Janet lifted both brows as she made her way into the kitchen. "Now, that could be interesting. We did talk to some of my customers from the bakery, but not about Dani's issues. It was something else entirely, but they may have said something to someone."

"You've been to see Rick, but he drives a white Jeep. He loves that thing."

"Debbie and I both had the impression that Rick's a good businessman who keeps his work honest. I don't think he'd do anything underhanded. But Dani was having words with her brother when I got to the farm this afternoon to talk about her trials of my recipes—both of which turned out fine, by the way."

"Didn't doubt it for a moment, love." He reached for the cookie jar on the counter. Ian had a serious sweet tooth and staunchly supported Janet's baking efforts. "What were they fighting about?"

"Whether they should sell the farm. I didn't hear everything that was said, but Dean seemed angry when he left. I think Dean also has some resentment toward his father. He feels underappreciated for the work he does around the farm."

Ian chewed a cookie thoughtfully. "Family stuff can escalate, but I've known Dean a long time. He's a pretty low-key guy. Doesn't ruffle easily."

"He was definitely mad today."

"We all get mad." Ian leaned against the counter. "Opportunities only knock so often. We've gotten through a lot of tough financial times in this town, and maybe Dean has that 'strike while the iron is hot' mentality. If that's the case, he's not wrong."

She'd opened the refrigerator to retrieve the pork chops she meant to prepare for dinner, but she spun to face him in shock. "You think they should sell the farm? Really?"

He held up his hands. "No. I like what they've done. But it's not my thoughts that matter. It's not even Dani's or Dean's. Whether to sell the farm or not is still their parents' decision. I'm sure that's frustrating, especially if Dean's worried about their age and whether they can keep up with the work. He probably takes their need for his help as confirmation that they can't."

His phone rang, interrupting their conversation. He took the call, and his expression darkened. "I'll be right there." He hung up and gave Janet a quick kiss on the cheek. "Sorry, honey, I have to go. Elderly male, possible heart attack."

Janet was used to him rushing off at the drop of a hat. "Okay. Keep me posted."

He hurried out.

Janet let out their Yorkshire terrier, Laddie, then put the pork chops away and heated up some leftover soup instead. She found Ranger, their dark gray cat, asleep on a kitchen chair and gave him some scratches while she waited for the soup.

Less than an hour later, Ian texted her. IT'S DANI'S FATHER. PROGNOSIS IS GOOD. NOT HEART EPISODE, BUT THEY DID DETECT A PROBLEM AND ARE KEEPING HIM TO BE EXAMINED BY A CARDIOLO- GIST TOMORROW. THEY SAID HIS INDIGESTION TONIGHT MIGHT HAVE SAVED HIS LIFE.

THAT'S GREAT NEWS, she texted back. THANK YOU FOR TELLING ME. BE BACK SOON.

She got a bowl of soup ready to heat up for him. Late nights in police work weren't uncommon, but the thought of a health problem for Mr. Addison added new fuel to an already smoking fire. Janet wasn't sure what could be done about that.

Helping people was in her nature, but sometimes you had to let go and let God do His work, His way. She was guilty of forgetting that too often.

But she'd help Dani in any way she could. After all, perhaps God's way could be worked through her.

# CHAPTER EIGHT

When Paulette took over the front of the café the next morning, Janet used the opportunity to fill Debbie in on Mr. Addison's health scare.

Debbie reacted much as Janet had. "Talk about one thing compounding the other."

"I know. I suggested to Dani that she talk to her father about Dean's building frustration with him, so I've been a bit worried that she followed my advice, and the stress sparked the whole issue." Janet began piping icing onto a row of carrot cake bars, a popular fall item in their area. "I'm sure I'm simply being paranoid, but I can't help wondering until I hear from her about it."

"Family tensions can cause all kinds of problems, though I never thought of them causing physical ones. But it makes sense. Stress can certainly cause health issues." Debbie finished a trio of orders for a group of local women who treated themselves to a café breakfast once a month. She added a small cookie to the side of each order.

Janet lifted a brow in question.

"Coming here once a month is the only fun those ladies allow themselves on their tight budgets." Debbie said. "I like adding a little bit to make it even more special."

"You're so thoughtful," Janet said. Paulette smiled when she spotted what Debbie had done. It was clear Debbie had won her approval as well.

"It's no big deal." Debbie brushed off the compliment as she threw home fries onto the grill for the next orders. Janet winked at Paulette.

When Janet went out front to set the carrot cakes in the bakery display case, the joy on those three women's faces added light to the room.

Then she got a text from Kim. DESPERATELY SEEKING HOT MOCHA LATTE. BIGGEST YOU'VE GOT. IT SEEMS THAT TRAVEL AROUND THANKSGIVING HAS BECOME EVEN CRAZIER THAN USUAL THIS YEAR AND FAMILY IS HAVING A HARD TIME MAKING AFFORDABLE CHOICES. WHY DIDN'T I THINK TO CELEBRATE THANKSGIVING IN SUMMER WHEN TRAVEL IS CHEAPER?

Janet sent her a swift reply. WE'LL REMEMBER THIS NEXT SUMMER. COME ON OVER. I'LL HAVE YOUR DRINK READY.

When Kim came through the door from the museum a few minutes later, Janet met her at the counter. "Your latte." She handed Kim the tall cup with the protective sleeve in place. "Extra hot, extra mocha. Sorry the whole Thanksgiving planning is such a mess."

"I'm trying not to stress over it."

Janet quirked a brow. "How's that working out for you?"

Kim sighed. "About as well as you'd expect, and it's my own fault. I put so much stock in this idea to gather everyone together because of Mom's age that every time I get a negative response, I feel like I'm letting Mom down. Which is ridiculous." She met Janet's gaze. "Intellectually I know that. Emotionally it's driving me crazy."

"Serenity Prayer time."

"You are totally right," Kim admitted. "It seems like having the wisdom to know the difference between what I can and can't change isn't as clear-cut as I'd like it to be."

"It seldom is," Janet said.

Kim rotated the cup in her hands. "It might be unfair, but the whole thing makes me mad. Why wouldn't people want to do everything they could to be here and celebrate? And then I realize that it's easy for me to say because I live here. I don't have to match schedules with college kids or basketball tournaments or any of the crazy things people have taking up space on their calendars in an already busy month. Besides, as the youngest, I'm pretty sure none of my older siblings want me bossing them around. I know at least one of them feels like that's what I'm doing. Maybe I am. They could even be more sensitive because they probably feel bad to miss it."

"I think Jim's advice the other day was solid," Janet said. "The accidents of time, weather, and finances are tough every holiday season. Focus on who *can* come. Then if people make it in at the last minute, there are lots of ways to stretch a turkey dinner."

"A few extra sides go a long way to feed an extra ten or twelve." Paulette had come up beside them to ring up the checks for the three elderly women. "Fresh rolls and butter too."

Kim laughed. "That is so true."

"And since everyone actually comes for dessert, we'll have you covered on that score." Janet promised cheerfully. "I'll adjust the order that week depending on the final count."

"Thank you, Janet." Kim's expression eased. "This is why I duck over here. Total and unequivocal understanding, plus perspective and workable solutions."

"Besides the fact that the door is mere steps from your office?" Paulette winked as she counted the women's change into three piles on the counter.

"Proximity has its benefits," Janet said.

"All true," Kim said, "but the camaraderie and support are what bring me in. You guys are the best. The great coffee and food are merely a fringe benefit, albeit a lovely one."

"Glad to hear it."

Kim left. As soon as she was out the door, Janet put in a quick call to Jim Watson.

She relayed her conversation with Kim, and the *Gazette* editor didn't disappoint. "I'll give her older brothers a call to see if there's any way to help get some of their crew here. Those guys aren't spring chickens themselves, but maybe hearing from an old friend will help."

Over the years people in Dennison and Uhrichsville had been able to count on Jim Watson's help for a multitude of things. No one was more appreciative of the editor's efforts than Janet and Ian. Jim had a way of getting to the bottom of things without causing offense, a wonderful trait. "I was hoping you'd say that. No one wants to be bossed around by the baby of the family."

Jim laughed. "Speaking as the oldest in my family, I will attest to the accuracy of your words. My baby sister is kind of a know-it-all."

"Well, brains run in the family, Jim."

He laughed again. "It's a birth order thing, I guess. Thanks for keeping me updated. Kim's brothers have been friends of mine for a long time. It would be good to see how their families are doing anyway."

She thanked him then ended the call and went back to refilling their bakery case. She pulled a couple of items that she'd drop off at the food bank on her way home, and when things calmed down a little after one, she called Dani.

"Hi, Dani. I wanted to see how your dad is doing. I heard last night that he had a spell, but I didn't want to intrude."

"It was crazy." Dani kept her voice low. "The heart doctor has been in to see him today, according to Mom. He ordered a whole bunch of tests to see what's going on. Mom's there, and I'm here running the farm. It's good for me to stay busy because otherwise I'd just be spiraling."

"I get that, but running the whole farm on your own?" Janet asked. The Addisons were usually a trio during the busy planting, growing, and harvest seasons, but especially now when sales hit the all-time annual highs.

"I have a little extra help, and that's a blessing," Dani assured her. "We'll be fine. But my brother made it a point to blame the farm and inadvertently me for Dad's episode or whatever it is. He says the stress of running a place like this would kill anyone, and he doesn't want it to be his father. It was a gruesome scene. I know most of it is pent-up anger and old hurt feelings, but it did make me realize that maybe Dean is more upset about the whole thing than I thought."

"Health scares raise the stakes, for sure."

"They do. He's clearly worried about Dad, and now that they've discovered a blocked vessel, I think maybe Dean's right. He told me that Dad will never walk away from the farm, even if I buy them out, because he loves this place. He said Dad will stay and work himself to death, and he asked if I want that on my conscience. It made me think, Janet." She took a deep breath and let it out. "He could be right. And he could be angry enough to sabotage things, although I would have never thought that was possible. I still can't wrap my head around it, but then I've never seen it so clearly from Dean's perspective before."

"These are huge family decisions, Dani."

"They sure are." Dani hesitated then went on. "But in the end, they should be *our* decisions. Me. Mom and Dad. We're the ones directly involved, and that should be where the decision lies, right? It's not that I don't value my brother's opinion, but he's always hated farming. It's not like that's some big secret. He didn't like working in all kinds of conditions, and he hated how dependent we were on good weather. The lack of control aggravated him. I also have this nagging thought that he doesn't trust me because I'm a woman."

"Has he said that?" The idea surprised Janet. Dean's wife ran a fine carpentry business, not exactly a traditionally feminine occupation.

"No. I expect he'd have doubts even if I were a man, but it's a shame he doesn't realize that I handle more than fifty percent of the farm already. Dad runs the tractors and a lot of the equipment, but I'm the go-to person who does all the ordering, organizing, market-ing, and social media, on top of my share of planting and harvest-ing. He might not know that, but if I tell him, it will strengthen his argument that Dad should give it up and retire."

"What would your dad's response be?"

"Dad's made it clear that he intends to die with his boots on. But he always adds that he's not aiming to see heaven for a while yet, God willing."

Janet had no answers, but she did have a suggestion. "I think it's time to divide and conquer, Dani. You focus on the farm. Let your mom focus on getting your dad well with the help of the doctors. All of you buckle down and concentrate on getting through this season. There's less than six weeks left."

The farm closed for the season at noon on Christmas Eve each year. Once closed, the Addisons took a well-deserved few days off before cleaning and clearing the barn so it would be ready for their strawberry season opening.

"Don't look any further than that for now," Janet went on. "It will be much easier to reason all of this out during the January lull. Calmer heads will prevail then, and that's the kind you want making these future plans. There's no rush to do anything or make decisions now, is there?"

"No. But having so many things going wrong stokes the fire. It's a constant concern."

Janet kept her tone firm. "Debbie and I will keep checking things out, and we'll update you regularly."

Dani let out a long breath. "Yes. It's good advice. We'll focus on what needs to be done here, and I'll leave the other in your hands. We've got this, Janet."

"You bet we do. Every business wants to make the most of those fourth-quarter sales," Janet said. "Keep me posted on how your dad is doing, and we'll keep you in the loop from our side. Okay?"

"Okay. Thanks, Janet."

"Anytime." They said their goodbyes, and Janet disconnected the call.

The café was empty, and the museum was quiet. Paulette had gone home while Janet was on the phone. Debbie was putting the final touches on cleanup, and Janet had put in her baking supplies order, so she took the window of time to do some research on her phone.

The Karras family who had lived near Lori Rosen had been gone a long while. Emily and Tom Brinkman were listed as the current owners of record. Emily was the daughter of Bill and Genevieve Karras, Letitia's youngest son and his first wife. Gen had passed away when Emily was in middle school. Her father remarried a few years later and moved away. Emily had finished school, married, and returned to Ohio nearly twenty years later. She and Tom had bought Letitia's old house, and all three of them now lived at that address.

"Hey." She poked her head through the kitchen door. "Do you have time to swing by Lettie Karras's place once we're done?"

"Can we keep our visit under an hour?" Debbie asked. "The boys are going winter shopping with Paulette, and Greg and I are going out to dinner."

Janet smiled. "How lovely."

Debbie looked a little less certain.

Janet moved into the kitchen while Debbie finished wiping down her counter area. "It's not nice?"

"That's just it." Debbie leaned back against the counter. "We have a really good time together, and we like each other—a lot. I see what kind of man he is, how good he is, how blessed those boys are to have him guiding their way, but then I wonder what my role is in all of this."

"What do you mean?" Janet asked.

"They had a mother," Debbie explained. "A good one. She's gone, and I don't know if kids are ever ready to have someone try to fill their mother's shoes. But how do you step into a man's heart and not be a parent to his children? I don't know what the boundaries are for any of that, and it worries me. No one wants to be the evil stepmother, right?"

"Right." Janet leaned against the other counter and faced her. "So don't be evil."

Debbie laughed, but it wasn't an easy laugh. "I suppose I could try that."

"I'm serious." Janet stayed practical. "Just be yourself. Be kind and respectful, and be there when they need you. I think you'll be surprised by how successful that will be."

"But how do I know when to keep quiet?" Debbie asked. "How do I know when to take a back seat?"

"That's a conversation you and Greg need to have," Janet said. "It's not the boys themselves who make you nervous. It's fearing you might do something wrong and upset them and Greg, when you care about all of them so much." She laid a hand on her friend's arm.

Debbie gave her a small smile. "I think that's exactly it."

"There's no perfect guide for kids. It's a learn-as-you-go endeavor, but I think if parents keep faith, hope, and love alive, kids can weather most battles that come their way. Tiffany did." She straightened. "You ready?"

"Let's go." Debbie grabbed her jacket. "How about if we drop your car at your place and I'll drive to Lettie's?"

"Perfect."

Soon, they pulled up to the Karras house on its quiet street. A group of small homes filled a good section of the block. Lettie's place was distinguished by brick steps and an olive-green front door. Spots of lichen on the steps spoke to the building's age, but the door's paint looked fresh, and everything was neat and tidy. Janet and Debbie went to the door and knocked.

No one answered, and there was no doorbell in view.

Janet knocked again.

Still nothing. She was about to lament not being able to contact anyone in the house when the sound of a window opening drew their attention upward.

An older woman peered at them from above. "I'm not giving, I'm not taking, and I'm not alone. There are plenty of people here to keep me safe, so you be on your way."

"Mrs. Karras?" Janet waved up to her. "It's Janet from the Third Street Bakery. You used to order three dozen chocolate chip cookies from us every month or so, and I made your grandson's first birthday cake, remember? The one with all the frosting balloons?"

The woman's countenance changed instantly. "That's right. That cake was delicious!" She made the pronouncement as if it were something much grander than a one-year-old's smash cake. "And those cookies were the best ever."

"It's the butter," Janet told her. "Use salted butter. No margarine or shortening. That's the secret."

"But you closed the bakery." The elderly woman's voice brimmed with reprimand. "I came back here expecting some things to be different, but I sure do miss those cookies."

"I brought a dozen along, actually. I wasn't sure if you'd remember me, but I was pretty sure you'd remember the cookies. We came around to ask you about an old neighbor from a while back," Janet explained. "We won't stay long, but if you wouldn't mind answering a couple of questions, Debbie and I would be most grateful."

"Answers for cookies?" A look of delight swept the suspicion from the woman's face. "Sounds fair to me." She closed the window.

"Amazing," Debbie murmured. "Your baking literally opens doors, my friend."

Janet chuckled.

When Mrs. Karras let them in, her face was bright with delight. "I can't even remember the last time I got a surprise visit here." She made the exclamation as she ushered them into the small kitchen, which had been modernized recently but kept the old charm of a classic twentieth-century home. "Have a seat. Will you have a cup with me? I've got one of those single-serve systems that are all the rage now, so it won't take but a minute."

Janet declined politely. "We don't have that long today, but we'd love it if you could come down to the depot and visit us, Mrs. Karras."

"Lettie, please. And I'll have to arrange that sometime."

"I'm Janet, but you probably already knew that from my name tag at the old bakery. This is my friend Debbie Albright. We've opened a café in the depot. I have your chocolate chip cookies there all the time."

"That sounds lovely. Now you, young lady." She settled into the chair beside Debbie and patted her hand. "Is that your mother working over at the health place I go to now? Becca Albright?"

"It is, yes. She loves it there."

"She's a nice woman. She's very patient and helpful."

Janet slid the container of cookies over to Lettie.

Lettie accepted the gift with a joyful sigh. She lifted the box, traced her finger over the fall-themed label, and then brought her gaze back to Janet and Debbie. "A lot's changed since I've been away, but a lot hasn't. It certainly felt like coming home when the kids called to ask if I'd like to live with them here."

Janet knew for a fact that the "kids" were middle-aged, but she let it slide.

"I've got the little bedroom off to the side there." She pointed to the cottage-style living room beyond the kitchen. "It's just right for me now. Although when folks come unexpectedly, I head upstairs. You never know who might be waiting outside your house if you open a downstairs window, know what I mean?"

"Safety first," Debbie agreed.

"Exactly that." Lettie tapped a firm finger on the tabletop. "A woman alone during the day has to manage all sorts of things. I'm no stranger to managing my life, such as it is now. Not so much to fuss over when you don't go anywhere. But what was it you gals wanted to know?"

Janet pointed across the road. "Red Meyers's rental across the way."

"God rest his soul." Lettie put a hand to her heart. "He kept his places nice, and we never had a problem with tenants, because Red was good and so were they. I think some of them lived there longer than I lived here, if you can believe it. What about them?"

"Red's niece found a packet of letters when she was cleaning out that rental," Janet said. "There's no legible address or return address even, so we don't know who they should be given to. It seems a shame to throw them away. The stamp on some of them indicates they were sent sometime after the late sixties."

Lettie seemed genuinely puzzled. "Surely there's a salutation and a closing on them. You know, 'Dear Lettie' and then a name of who it's from. My fifth-grade teacher gave us firm instructions about writing a letter. 'Respectfully yours, Jason', or 'Sincerely, Letitia.' We did things properly then, and the art of writing letters wasn't taken casually."

"No name." Janet didn't hide her regret. "They all begin with 'My dearest wife,' and end with 'your loving husband.'"

Lettie's look of confusion deepened. "And they were found in that house over there?"

Janet and Debbie both nodded.

Lettie leaned back in her chair. "I can't for the life of me imagine who it could be, which probably sounds silly after decades, but there was never a married woman living alone in that house all the while I was here. Unless it's someone more recent, someone who lived there while I didn't live here."

Debbie shrugged. "It's hard to know. We only know for sure that they were there sometime since the late sixties."

"There were two families in that duplex in the sixties," Lettie mused. "The Osminkowskis lived on the left, and the Eidenbachs lived on the right. Both Eidenbachs passed on early, but their daughter Ann Marie lived there for decades. She's over at Good Shepherd now, I think. I heard that when Red passed and Ann Marie realized the place would be sold and changed, she decided to go to assisted living. Remove the stress of daily upkeep. She told them if she had to move, she'd move once. So that was that."

"How old was she in the sixties?"

"Little more than a teenager, about twenty or so. Quiet. Rather plain. I don't mean that in a mean way," Lettie hurried to say. "But she wasn't the kind of girl who seemed to attract attention from boys. She'd walk around with her eyes down, not looking around except to cross the street. I saw her often enough because she sorted things at the post office. Now they've got fancy machines to sort through things. Back then everything was done by hand."

"So every letter was hand-sorted then?"

"Yes ma'am." Lettie helped herself to a cookie but didn't bite into it. "Her mother once told me how they offered her a delivery route at one time. That was a step up. Ann Marie refused it. She told her mother that she preferred being behind the scenes, and I expect that was true."

"She was single? All that time?" Debbie asked.

"Still is, far as I know," Lettie said. "At least her last name hasn't changed, so I'm assuming she never married. Not that that's a guarantee, of course. Women not changing their names or putting a hyphen here, there, or wherever—there's nothing wrong with that, but it makes it a little harder to figure out the who's who of things."

"It does." Janet checked the time then met Debbie's gaze and stood. "Lettie, you've been a big help."

Lettie stood with them. "I'm not sure how, but it's been real nice to have company. My eyes aren't as good as they used to be, so I don't drive anymore, but my granddaughter will bring me by the depot to see what you girls are up to over there."

"We'd like that very much," Debbie told her.

"That depot is a shining star in our community," Lettie added. "So nice to have it all cleaned up, and so much history inside. I was a busy mom back when people rallied to purchase the depot and fix it up, but I helped on that committee. That depot, those trains, and what it all did for service members during World War II meant a lot to so many of us. It was our parents and grandparents who gathered to help send those men and women off to war, and they didn't take it lightly."

"As they shouldn't," Janet said as they stepped out the door.

"Thank you again for the visit," Lettie said. "I'll see you at the depot." She waved, then closed the door, and Janet heard the click of the lock.

Debbie and Janet crossed to the car. "We need to see Ann Marie Eidenbach," Debbie said. She glanced at her watch. "But not today. I have to get home."

"And get all gussied up for your big date?" Janet teased.

Debbie laughed. "Well, at least cleaned up, so I don't smell like a café grill."

"Valid point. I want to swing by Dean Addison's car repair shop at some point too. I think it might be easier to talk to him at work rather than at home. He might find talking with kids around uncomfortable. And I'd like to surprise him," Janet added. "Not blindside him, but I want to see his honest reaction to Dani's concerns."

"I can't imagine he'll appreciate being accused of sabotaging his family," Debbie noted in a dry tone as she took the bridge to the Dennison side of the creek.

"Exactly why we won't make him feel that way," Janet replied. "If we make it a fact-finding mission and ask his advice, it won't put him on the defensive. I hope."

# CHAPTER NINE

anet called Dani after supper that evening while Ian was out walking Laddie. The house was quiet. It had taken Janet a while to get used to a quieter house when Tiffany had gone off to school in Cleveland. She'd adjusted to the new normal, but she was excited that Tiffany and her friends would be home for a four-day weekend in two weeks. On one side of the kitchen table she had a list of what she needed for Thanksgiving and what she'd like to do with the girls.

On the other side was the page of notes she'd made of potential troublemakers for Claymont Creek Farm. None of them jumped out at her as more or less likely to be behind it all.

They hadn't talked with Charlie Briscoe yet. Or Dean, for that matter, but she'd watched enough crime shows to know that the three determining factors for solving any mystery were means, motive, and opportunity.

She understood Dean's possible motive. She'd witnessed his anger. He was familiar with everything about the farm, which gave him means and opportunity, but was he angry enough at his family to sabotage them?

They'd witnessed Hailey's antics and tracked her on the web. Claymont Creek Farm wasn't her only target. She was still a plausible suspect. They needed to check her out, so Janet made a note to reach out to other farms in the area. If Hailey was the culprit, she'd probably messed with more than one farm that used animal labor.

She crossed Rick Radner off the list. They'd liked him, and he seemed honest and aboveboard. He also had Ian's and Greg's seals of approval.

But if Rick wasn't involved, could there be an unknown developer vying for premium land in Dani's area? Or could Charlie Briscoe be carrying on the old family feud between his uncle Mitchell and Dani's father? If so, why? Charlie had never been that kind of guy when they were younger, but the intervening years could change a lot of things.

Had Mr. Addison done something to stir up old issues after Charlie took over the farm? Mack had witnessed Charlie's truck pulled off the road near the Addisons' place, so that offered opportunity, but Janet couldn't begin to guess at a motive. But then, she hadn't talked to Charlie in over twenty-five years, so anything was possible. For a guy schooled in financials, losing the farm's value could hit hard. But would that give him motive?

First things first. She checked the time, saw that Debbie wouldn't actually be on her date yet, and called her. "Do we have time to swing by Dean's mechanic shop on Monday afternoon?"

"He might not be there," Debbie replied. "The eighth-grade American history classes are giving their presentations of early Thanksgiving celebrations. Kelsey Addison is in Julian's class. I'm meeting Greg there at three. But you could come along with me and we'll see if he's there. If he's not, let's stop by his shop after the presentations wrap up. I don't want to corner him at school, but we could set up a time that works for him either way."

She'd checked Dean's hours on his website. He was open until six on Mondays, so that could work. "I'm in. I want to get to Good Shepherd to see Ann Marie Eidenbach next week too. We could take Ray and Eileen a few treats to share while we're there. Does that work for you?"

"You bet. We're in a lull between football and basketball, so we can head over to Good Shepherd right after we close on Tuesday."

"Perfect. But we can't let on to Eileen what Kim's planning," Janet reminded her friend. "If it works out, that is. I'd hate to let the cat out of the bag, especially if the surprise doesn't come together after all."

"Mum's the word. Also, FYI, the church hall is open Monday afternoon to accept donations for the clothing drive. I'm bringing a whole bunch to get that taken care of then too."

The church was doing a traditional clothing drive all month long. Their mothers, Lorilee Hill and Becca Albright, had arranged to gather items from neighbors and friends, but Janet hadn't been able to coordinate her schedule with theirs. This eliminated the need for that. "Put yours in the back of my car on Monday morning, and I'll drop them off with mine on my way to the school after work. That way you don't have to make an extra stop. It's more important for you to be on time anyway."

"Thank you," Debbie said. "Mom's idea to gather things to take in was wonderful. We got lots of stuff from folks that might not have gotten around to it otherwise, but her time frame has been choppy because of overtime at the clinic."

"And you're busy," Janet filled in for her.

"I thrive on being busy," Debbie said. "But it's possible I didn't factor in all the new aspects of my life when I came back home." She laughed. "I wouldn't change a thing, but I'm happy to accept that favor."

As Janet hung up, she reflected on Debbie's words. She didn't think she'd change a thing either.

Janet left the café a few minutes early on Monday afternoon. It gave her time to call her parents and wish them a happy anniversary before she lugged the donation bags into the church's gathering hall.

Brenda Winston, Pastor Nick's wife, oversaw the center, and she flashed Janet a smile. "Do you have more?"

"Loads more. I brought Debbie's donations with me as well."

"Wonderful." Brenda grabbed a lunchroom cart and began pushing it to the door. "Do you want to get the other one?"

"Perfect." Janet followed her out with a second cart. As they loaded Brenda's with half a dozen big bags, Janet said, "This is so much easier, Brenda."

"Agreed. We bought three of these carts on a whim at a garage sale a couple of years ago, and it's amazing how often they get used. The garage sale fundraiser, the clothing drive, lunches or snacks for youth group. It was the best investment because it saves me time. You might not have guessed, but I'm in favor of anything that saves a pastor's wife time."

Janet laughed. "I concur. I'm heading over to the school presentations on American history. This way I'll get there a little early."

"Glad to help." The bags were marked with specific ranges of clothing to help organize the collection efforts. Janet moved her cart to the kids' section while Brenda steered hers into the winter use area. Thanks to the carts, they had unloaded and sorted the donations in no time.

Janet said goodbye to Brenda, got into her car, and headed for the school. When construction slowed traffic one way, she ducked down a side road to go around to the school from a different direction.

And there they were, right in front of her as she slowed for the stop sign.

Rick Radner and Charlie Briscoe, in a heated discussion.

Rick's face was red with anger.

Charlie appeared more determined than mad. He folded his arms—which were still large, indicating that he'd kept up his physical health since his quarterbacking days—and clearly refused to back down.

Janet couldn't stop to try to figure out more. She was already holding up a car behind her, but as she made the turn toward the school, she noticed another thing.

A black SUV.

Was it Charlie's? And was it the same one that had been waiting in her driveway a few days before?

After she parked, she pulled up her phone's internet browser—and found herself learning more about Charlie Briscoe than she could have imagined. Charlie hadn't simply been a financial advisor in Chicago. He'd become CFO of a major investment firm. When she saw the seven-figure salary believed to be associated with Charlie's former position, her mouth fell open.

Charlie wasn't just well-off. He was rich.

So yeah, he might be upset about the farm not working out initially, but would it drive a rich man to low-end shenanigans like what was happening at the Addison farm?

Her first guess was no, but Mack had seen Charlie's vehicle pulled off the road in the vicinity of Claymont Creek Farm. She'd seen him with Rick. Was Rick trying to buy the Briscoe farm? It had proximity to Claymont Creek Farm and the towns. Charlie's family farm was conveniently situated between two country roads. That meant Charlie's property had a lot of road frontage, an important part of neighborhood planning.

But why would that make Charlie angry? Wouldn't a simple "not interested" end that discussion?

Someone tapped on her window.

She jumped, startled.

Debbie was outside the car. She pointed to her watch.

Janet silenced her phone and tucked it away. She climbed out of the car, and the two women went to meet Greg at the edge of the parking lot.

Greg greeted them warmly and then pressed a kiss to Debbie's temple.

Janet made a show of scanning the area around them. "Aren't you missing someone? Maybe with four legs and thick black-and-white fur?"

Greg laughed. "You're right. Hammer probably would have gotten a lot out of these presentations."

"Even border collies have the right to learn American history," Janet said with mock sternness as they walked inside.

Janet didn't see Dean at the presentation, but his wife, Amelia, was there. She held her phone up and recorded Kelsey's well-written essay as the eighth grader read it to the gathered crowd. The audience's applause was genuine and heartfelt.

Julian's report was quite different. He made the gathering laugh at his humorous rendition of finding the best turkey in the wilderness, making sure it was not too big or too small. He drew more laughs when he reenacted Pilgrims selecting only the ripest cranberries and trying to ascertain which squash had the thickest neck. Then he brought the house down when he explained how colonists boiled meat bones to achieve enough gelatin for what might have been the first shredded carrot-and-gelatin salad to be left uneaten at a holiday dinner table.

To make his point, Julian had made his version of "Sunshine Salad" in a round mold, centered on a plain wooden tray. He added a date card to the display: *1621—and still uneaten.*

When the program was over, Greg wrapped an arm around him. "I didn't know they made gelatin back then."

"Not the box form," Julian explained. "The boil-the-bones type. Debbie explained it to me, and I was all weirded out until I realized that's how this treasure of a salad might have been born." He grinned broadly. "I think if we voted on least likely to be eaten at anyone's Thanksgiving table, this would be it. Especially if they used lemon-flavored gelatin."

Greg laughed. "I can't disagree. Your mom's mom always made some kind of gelatin-based dish that she said was her own mother's recipe."

"Hey, there are some amazing gelatin dishes," Debbie told them. "Pretzel-bottom gelatin is one of my favorites. My mom has made that for every party we've ever had, and it's wonderful."

Julian and Greg exchanged dubious looks.

"I'll have Mom make a small one for Thanksgiving," she told them. "It's one of my favorite desserts. Strawberries, cream cheese, and a crunchy pretzel-crust bottom. Delicious."

Julian wrinkled his nose at the unappetizing gelatin mold on his breadboard. Then he raised his gaze to Debbie's. "I'll try it. But only because your mom is making it and I don't want to hurt her feelings. She did let me borrow her mold, after all."

They all burst out laughing as they headed to the exit.

A few minutes later, Janet and Debbie swung by Addison Auto Repair. The closed garage doors blocked the worst of the wind, but Dean and his two mechanics still worked in a chilly setting. He spotted them as they passed through the small office area. He stood and came their way. "Car trouble, ladies?"

"Not at all," Janet said. "You keep my car in great shape."

He tilted his head, clearly puzzled. "Then how can I help you?"

Janet glanced around to make sure no one was listening. "I don't know if this is a good time or place to have this discussion."

"About?"

"The farm."

The two words changed his expression, which went from open and inquisitive to completely shut down and slightly forbidding. "I'm not part of the farm. It's not a topic of conversation I want to open. But why would the two of you come here to talk about that? Is my dad still having medical trouble?"

"Not that I've heard," Janet told him. "But someone is messing with things at the farm. Nothing dangerous—at least not yet. But random acts of vandalism can wear a person down, and I know

Dani's worried but trying to keep it from your parents as much as possible so they don't worry."

He gaped at her. "Someone is vandalizing our farm?"

Janet didn't miss his switch to the inclusive pronoun. *Interesting that he says he's not a part of it but then immediately calls it "our" farm.*

"Are they breaking things? Graffiti? What are we talking about, and why hasn't Dani told me? I get why she doesn't want our parents to worry, but I could help her." He paused for a moment, and then realization dawned. "She thinks I would do something like that? For real?"

Janet backtracked quickly. "She's not asking that at all, Dean. We are. I saw you at the farm last week. You were extremely angry."

"So you think I'd do something to hurt my parents and my sister? To compromise their already shaky future?"

Janet kept her voice calm. "I know you've had words with Dani lately. She told us because we jumped in to help when her ovens broke down. She's worried that someone is deliberately causing trouble."

"What's been happening?" he demanded.

Debbie ticked things off on her fingers. "They've dealt with deliberately clogged plumbing, a missing log splitter, cut fencing—"

"Recently?" Dean cut in.

Janet nodded. "Within the past month or so. And I honestly didn't know if your feelings toward your father—"

Dean broke in. "I love my father, but he's been known to take advantage of a situation when he sees an opportunity. He'd probably deny that, but it's true. Part of my concern is seeing Dani spend her whole life working there, staying the course when she could be doing other things, living her own life rather than the one he wants her to live. It doesn't make sense to me. She's smart enough to be anything she wants, and yet she stays there, slogging in the dirt day after day, year after year."

"Running one of the area's most popular businesses," Debbie reminded him. "There's a lot to be said for a woman running a farm. Or a carpentry business."

"I'm not against women in business," Dean clarified. "I don't want to see Dani wind up with the short end of the stick and nothing to show for it. Dad loves us, but he loves his farm more. If he decides to sell, he's not about to give over a portion of that to Dani to give her a fresh start. That's not how he does things. Trust me." He glanced around the business he'd built from the ground up. "I know. But that's a different conversation and nothing we need to talk about now. I want to know who's messing with the farm. I can tell you that it's not me."

Janet believed him. "We don't know who it is. Maybe a developer who's after land around here. Maybe a distraught patron."

"Or that animal woman."

Debbie's brows went up. "Hailey? You know Hailey?"

"My son has filled me in on what she's been doing there. He's seen it often enough. She's also been trashing our farm and others on social media. Someone tagged my wife in one of the posts so she could see what's happening, and it's ridiculous. Hailey has even drawn up a petition to stop them from using the donkeys to pull the carts. Why can't people mind their own business?"

Janet couldn't answer that for him. "We saw the police having a chat with Hailey a week or so ago. She's definitely on the short list of people who might hold a grudge against the farm, as silly as that sounds to people who love the place."

"Make sure I'm off that list, please," Dean said. "I might have differences with my father, and we both might be too stubborn for our own good, but I'll stand shoulder to shoulder with my parents and my sister against any more damage. There's no reason for that. My family has worked that land for eighty years now. If my parents decide to sell, that's fine. A part of me wishes they would because it causes Dad too much stress, but the other part of me knows he lives for the stress. He likes to feel victorious over the weather, the bugs, the blights. It's crazy to me when there are so many other options, but he and Dani seem suited to it. Although his age is showing."

"You mean with the heart condition?" Janet suggested.

"Yeah. He walks slower these days too. Farming is hard on the body, and he's not one to go and get those things addressed if he can help it. I did go off the deep end about his health when they put him in the hospital, but then my wife reminded me that she lost her father when she was sixteen years old and that we don't number our days. God does." He grimaced. "It was a valid reminder to get off my high horse, so I went over to my parents' place this morning and apologized."

"You did?"

He shoved his hands into the pockets of his grease-marked overalls. "I owed them that. My dad is a curmudgeon, but he's earned the right to run his own life. I should be supporting that, not condemning it."

It was a gentlemanly move for someone whose income was directly affected by his father's ways. After all, Dean kept buying supplies and making repairs, without any reimbursement. If Dean was willing to make amends and move on, Janet respected him for it.

"I'll call Dani this evening and remind her that I'm on her side. I don't think I've made that clear enough the last couple of years, and that's on me. I simply assumed she knew it, and I didn't realize she needs me to say it. I'll be better about that in the future."

"I'm glad to hear it," Janet told him. "Thanks for your time, Dean."

"Thanks for telling me what's really going on," he replied, and he went back to work.

Janet waited until they got into the car before she turned to face Debbie. "Well?"

"Quite the conversation," Debbie observed.

It sure was. Janet pulled out her phone and crossed Dean off her list of people to see. "I'm glad he's trying to make amends. But I do wish his dad would pay him. I can't think why he wouldn't."

"It doesn't make sense," Debbie agreed. "But a lot of things that people do don't make sense, so that's just added to the list. Since we're over this way, should we run by Good Shepherd and check out Miss Eidenbach?"

Janet shook her head. "The first dinner seating is at five. I'd hate to interrupt her meal. Are you still good for tomorrow?"

"Yes."

Janet backed out of her parking space. "I passed by an interesting scene on my way over to the school today. Rick Radner and Charlie Briscoe having a heated discussion in Rick's front yard."

Debbie arched her left brow. "For real?"

"Yes ma'am. And I got the impression Charlie was standing his ground over something. I checked him out online, and I'm pretty sure he isn't hurting for money. He left his job after making a seven-figure salary for over a dozen years."

"Whoa." Debbie didn't hide her surprise. "So needing time for the farm to do well isn't quite the issue we thought it was."

"Exactly." Janet steered onto the road. "But people behave in strange ways sometimes. We've seen that often enough."

"True words. So maybe Rick was honest about not targeting the Addison property. Maybe he's been hounding Charlie for the Briscoe farm instead."

Janet was thinking the very same thing. "Using the farm's struggles as leverage to get him to sell, maybe?"

"And you never tell a good quarterback to give up the game. That's one lesson I've learned from Greg and the boys. You stay in the game until the clock runs out, because you never know when the tables could turn."

"That's true in a lot of cases."

Dusk had fallen, and as they passed the new ice-skating rink behind the town's gazebo, the lights flickered on. Overhead lighting and twinkling strings made the new rink a central focus between Grant Street and the depot. The highway department had been hanging wreaths on the vintage-style lampposts that had been installed two years before, and the combination of the holiday greens and bright lights offered a festive addition for their historic little town.

"I love the rink and the lighting. They cleaned up the gazebo and incorporated all of it together so well. Look at the people lining up to skate." Debbie indicated a group heading into the small rink office. "It's wonderful to see new things bringing people together."

Dennison's officials were working hard to rejuvenate the town's appearance while keeping its vintage charm and connection to its history. They'd applied for multiple grants over the past several years, and Dennison was reaping the benefits of those efforts now. "It's amazing, isn't it?" Janet agreed. "I wonder if all this was spurred by Rick's campaign to fix up places, providing more street appeal and more reason to buy in Dennison?"

"One thing inspires the next and so on."

"Exactly. We might be part of it too, taking over the café when we did, putting a fresh spin on an aging facade. It all fits, with these things giving each other momentum."

Debbie nodded. "My decision to move home and put the city behind me. Grab a fresh start."

Janet smiled. "Well, you've outdone yourself on that one."

"Unexpectedly." Debbie grinned. "But it's quite welcome. I had no thoughts of romance when I decided to leave Cleveland. Just thoughts of something new in a familiar place with people I care about. Your baking experience made the café a no-brainer. I love to run things, and you love to bake. Making good coffee was as simple as finding a great supplier. It really came together, didn't it?"

"The timing was perfect for me too, and I love what we've made." Janet pulled into Debbie's driveway. "Thanks for coming with me today."

"Will you need help with that big muffin order in the morning?" Debbie asked.

"No, I'm going in early to get them done and packaged. The November orders are stacking up, and I need to check my supply list against the Thanksgiving week orders. I love the uptick in business, but those ovens are going to be hopping for the next month or so."

"Check out the sky when you go in," Debbie advised. "The Leonids meteor showers are peaking this week. Greg mentioned it. I once watched the Leonids with a stargazer group in Cleveland. I remember doing that when we were in Girl Scouts together. The

Cleveland group wasn't too serious, but when you live on the shores of a Great Lake, seeing the stars and the storms roll in is pretty cool."

"Do you miss it?" Janet asked. Debbie had done a complete one-eighty on her corporate life in Cleveland, and every now and again Janet wondered if she regretted the decision to move back home.

Debbie put that thought to rest swiftly. "Not at all. I had my fill of interoffice drama and dog-eat-dog corporate types. I accomplished my goals and was still young enough to change course, so I did a whole lot of praying. In the end, it wasn't about being successful. I'd achieved that. It was about finding joy, and I'm so glad I have." She gave a peaceful sigh as she climbed out of the car. "God's timing, right?"

"It never fails. See you tomorrow." Janet backed out of the driveway, gave Debbie one last wave, and headed home.

Full dark had fallen by the time she pulled into her driveway. The outside lights were on. Laddie scampered to greet her when she let herself in the side door, jumping around her legs and yipping with delight.

Ranger ignored her and the dog, barely stirring from his nap on the back of Ian's recliner, one of his favorite haunts. It was a peaceful night.

Until Ian's phone rang at twenty past two in the morning. He always tried to be considerate with overnight callouts. He'd slip out of bed, grab his things, and tiptoe to the door as quietly as he could.

That rarely worked because of Laddie's need to warn the entire house of strange noises. Tonight was no exception, and by the time Ian was out the door, Janet was wide awake. She'd planned to go in early to fill the big muffin order, but her wake-up time for that was an hour away yet.

She drew a breath, realized she'd never get back to sleep, and headed downstairs. She had enough time to grab coffee and plan her Thanksgiving shopping list before she needed to get to the café.

Except Dani called a few minutes later. She answered the call at once, alarmed by what could be causing it at this hour. "Dani? What's wrong?"

Anger and frustration hiked her old friend's voice. "The frame that protects our decorations by the road is burning. The fire department's here. So is Ian. I tried to put it out with a hose, but it wouldn't reach. The best it would do was wet down the area on my side so the fire didn't spread."

"How awful!"

"Yes, but Janet, I smelled gasoline. There was no mistaking it. The odor hung in the air like a blanket. Someone's not simply trying to annoy us. They're trying to scare us. I can tell you right now it's working."

Tiny hairs rose up on Janet's neck. Arson wasn't minor mischief. Arson was violent and dangerous, and whoever this was—if it was one person—had upped their game substantially. "You're sure you smelled gas?"

"I'm positive. Ian's talking to my parents. He and the fire chief are going to investigate because the fire chief smelled it too. Someone set that frame on fire deliberately. We want to know who."

# CHAPTER TEN

The fire department had doused the flames by the time Janet pulled into the Addisons' driveway twenty minutes later. This time the miscreant had gone too far. Fire wasn't merely destructive. It could be deadly, and that wasn't something the local police and fire departments would take lightly.

Inside the house, Ian interviewed Dani's parents while Dani stood nearby.

Janet poked her head through the door and caught Dani's eye. Dani quickly joined her. It was cold outside, so they stepped onto the enclosed porch that overlooked the sprawling farmyard.

Janet hugged her friend. "I'm so sorry. How are your parents doing?"

"Not well," Dani admitted. "Dad is beside himself. He and Uncle Royce built those frames when you and I were still in grade school. The structures have stood here for years, storm after storm. Now the far one is gone. Totally destroyed. Thank God it wasn't near anything else that could catch fire. I can't imagine how bad this could have been if it were windy tonight."

Janet sucked in a breath at the idea. "And they're pretty sure it's arson?"

Dani scowled. "Yes. They smelled gas, and there's a trail of burnt grass that followed the person or the gas can for about two dozen feet. Then it vanished."

"Because he or she probably realized it was leaking and didn't want to leave a trail back to their home or the road or whatever."

"That's what the fire chief said." A tear slid down her cheek. "Oh, what a mess, Janet. This is dangerous. It's like something out of a dramatic movie, and I can't for the life of me imagine who would want to shut us down that badly. Or scare us. I can't think of who we could have offended. Even with Dad's stick-in-the-mud ways, there's no one with this kind of a grudge against him."

Janet staged her next question carefully. "Is your dad still annoyed with the Briscoes? Even after they sold the farm to Charlie?"

Dani considered it. "Dad doesn't give up his grudges easily, but he doesn't do anything about them. He just grumbles. Plus, Charlie isn't anything like his uncle. My father should realize that, but he's still bitter over things that happened thirty years ago. If your last name is Briscoe, my father gives you a wide berth. It's ridiculous."

"And you don't think Charlie could be behind any of this?"

Dani's mouth fell open. "Charlie? No, of course not. Why would you think that?"

Janet started to answer, but then her watch beeped a reminder that she needed to head to the depot and get pumpkin muffins in the oven. "I'm glad to hear it. I'm trying to check all the boxes. I wouldn't imagine Charlie having anything against your family or your dad either, but this all started happening after he bought the Briscoe farm. And I don't know him these days."

"I expect he's every bit as nice and hardworking as the young man we knew back in the day. You can take him off your list, Janet. I'm sure he'd never do anything of the kind," Dani said firmly. "But I understand we owe you our thanks for something else. Dean came by last evening, and we all had a long, productive talk. I think we understand each other a little better now. He's going to be livid when he hears about this. I worry that this person might step up their game even more. I couldn't live with myself if anything happened to Mom or Dad."

"I'm sure they feel the same way about you." Janet pulled a pack of tissues from her purse and handed it to her friend. "No one wants this to escalate, but it seems that whoever's doing this is going for exactly that."

Dani's father burst onto the porch. "I'm installing cameras today. We'll put an end to this nonsense once and for all. Dean told me to do it years ago, and I didn't listen, but I'm going to fix that right away."

Agnes followed him out. "Calm down," she ordered. She planted her hands on her hips. "I'll set up a meeting with the security team Ian recommended once it's open. But it's not going to do much good if we end up burying the farmer because he wasn't mindful of his heart as his doctors ordered him to be. In the meantime, Ian and some others are putting hunting cameras around. That might get us through until we can set up a more permanent solution. They're camouflaged, so they'll barely be noticeable."

Dani's dad opened his mouth as if to say something. One stern glare from his wife squelched that.

Janet turned back to Dani. "I've got to get down to the depot, but I want you to know you're not alone in this. Any of you." She gave Dani another hug and whispered, "We'll figure things out."

Dani didn't reply except to hug her tighter.

When Janet was on her way to the depot, Ian called. He wasted no time in issuing a concerned husband warning. "I know you want to help Dani," he said, "but this guy has upped the ante, and I don't want anything to happen to you or Debbie because you put your-selves in the crosshairs with the Addisons."

"It won't," she protested.

"The arson team is going to check this out. The police are fol-lowing up. Let us do our jobs, okay? I don't want anyone hurt. If this person feels like they're under the microscope, they could become dangerous. Arson is high on the crime list, Janet. And don't forget that the Addisons didn't report all of the lesser things because they didn't want people to know there was a problem. Now we're on the case, and there's a whole lot to dig through."

"And that's so good to know," she answered brightly as she pulled into the parking lot behind the skating rink. "This way we can help each other. After you write this up, why don't you come by for coffee?"

He sighed, understanding her response perfectly—she and Debbie would keep their quiet inquiry going. But he also knew she was good at figuring things out for herself, a skill learned through a love of mysteries and being a police chief's wife.

"I'll take you up on that coffee." His tone was resigned.

She had the muffins baked and packaged by the time Debbie arrived a little after six o'clock. Janet had just filled her in when Ian came through the café door about ten minutes later.

She handed him a coffee, and Debbie poured one for herself. They gathered in the kitchen area.

"I'm going to interview neighbors later this morning," Ian said. "See if anyone saw or heard anything, but I'm going to reiterate my warning to you two. This person, whoever he or she is, is escalating their behavior. Fire is nothing to take lightly."

"But they were cautious enough to do it on a night without a speck of wind," Janet reminded him. "Couldn't that mean they didn't want to risk it spreading?"

"Be that as it may—"

"I'm not saying it isn't serious," she pressed. "It is. But a cold, damp night with no wind is the perfect time to start a fire that you don't want to spread. They picked the most noticeable structure, the one farthest from the house and closest to the road. It was spotted quickly, even in the middle of the night. Who called it in?"

He shook his head. "It was an anonymous tip."

"Does that mean it could have been the arsonist?" Debbie asked.

"It could have been," Ian acknowledged. "Especially if he or she didn't want to cause extensive damage and merely wanted to send a warning."

"Warning received," Janet said.

"Agreed. And I'm going to repeat myself to you two: use caution." Ian eyed both of them sternly. "I'd prefer if you stopped altogether, but I know you too well to think you'll give up when your friend is in danger."

"You've got that right," Janet said.

"But we will be careful," Debbie added. "We have too much going on these next two months to get too risky. How did Dani handle the whole thing?"

Janet set the oven temperature for pies, though baking wouldn't get her full attention today. Her brain was working the possibilities of who might be targeting a nice family like the Addisons. Unfortunately, her thoughts were coming up blank.

"About the way you'd expect," Janet told her. "Not badly, and not in front of her parents, but you can tell it hit her hard."

"That might be a good thing," Ian said. "This forced them to get us involved more fully. We knew about the log-splitter theft back in September, and we have the nuisance complaints on Hailey, but we didn't have the whole picture until Clint filled me in. I knew what you had told me, but it wasn't in my jurisdiction until they were ready to lodge a complaint. Now it's official. That frees my hands considerably."

Debbie started the grill for home fries. Crispy home-fried potatoes were a big deal on cold mornings. "Having you on board might be exactly what we've needed to gain some insight, Ian."

"This person seems to do most of their work at night, so having cameras on hand could be the answer," Janet added.

"Clint's getting camera security installed?" Debbie winced. "I hate that it's come to this, that a family business can't simply exist peacefully in a town like ours. That makes no sense to me, but even worse is that we have no idea who's responsible for the theft and vandalism. Who could hate the Addisons that much?"

"That's the problem." Ian finished his coffee. "No one hates them that we're aware of. Well, other than Mitchell Briscoe, Charlie's uncle, but he's gone. And why would an animal rights protestor like Hailey steal a log splitter or set fire to a structure? Those two things seem out of character for her, at least from what I know. I'll talk to the sheriff up in Sugarcreek because they've had to deal with her too. He might offer some insight." He rinsed his mug and set it beside the dishwasher. "Where did you say you gals were going after work?"

"Good Shepherd," Janet replied, and she didn't miss the relief that washed over his face. "Simple supper tonight."

"Frozen meatballs and a jar of your homemade pasta sauce?" Ian suggested. "Something hearty. We're doing a basketball workout at the middle school with Greg's boys and a handful of others. Gotta polish things up for the coming season."

"Perfect."

He pressed a kiss to her temple and headed for the door. "Love you. Please remember what I said about being careful."

"You know me," Janet said.

Ian paused in the kitchen doorway. "Yes, I do. If I didn't, I might feel more reassured."

# CHAPTER ELEVEN

T he museum hosted multiple school field trips that day. The overflow of people grabbing coffee or a quick soup-and-sandwich combo made the hours fly. Paulette stayed late to help with cleanup, which allowed Debbie and Janet to pull into Good Shepherd's parking lot a little before three.

The trees had lost the last of their leaves the week before, and the afternoon wind had picked up while they were inside. Winter cold was due to descend on the area overnight, and the uptick in wind and plummeting temperatures bore out the forecast. Janet and Debbie hurried into the center's welcoming warmth.

Receptionist Ashley Cramer greeted them as they came through the door. Her smile deepened when Janet handed her a wax paper sleeve of three freshly baked chocolate chip cookies. "What a treat! Thank you, Janet."

"You're most welcome." Janet met Ashley's smile with one of her own. "We have some for Ray and Eileen too—and for Ann Marie Eidenbach."

"Well, Ray and Eileen are watching a movie in the great room right now, and I don't dare interrupt."

"And we wouldn't want you to." Debbie indicated the cookie packages with a glance. "Would you be willing to see that they get them after the movie?"

"I'm happy to do that. Miss Eidenbach too?"

"That's who we've actually come to see," Janet said.

"How wonderful!" Ashley said. "I don't think we've ever logged a visitor for her that wasn't medical personnel. She just came out to the library cart in the solarium." The large, bright solarium was a popular gathering spot at Good Shepherd. "Does she know you?"

"Not yet," Janet hedged. "Her old house was being cleaned out by the new owners, and they found something that might be hers. They wanted to make sure it was returned to the right person."

"Oh, isn't that lovely?"

Janet wasn't sure about that, but she let it slide as Ashley led them to the solarium. She had them wait at the entrance as she crossed the spacious room. She paused at a straight-backed chair then bent over a white-haired woman sitting there.

The woman had an unopened book on her lap and wore a dour expression. Her scowl only deepened as Ashley spoke. Then she spotted Janet and Debbie. "Don't know 'em and don't care to. Stop bothering me with all your dithering, girl, or I'll report you to management. Again."

Her threat shocked Janet, but Ashley seemed unfazed. "You know I'm just doing my job, Miss Eidenbach. I have to check with you if you get a visitor."

"I don't get visitors."

"Then it sounds like today is your lucky day," Ashley said brightly. "They found something in your old house. They wanted to come see you about it and return it if you want it. That's all. Two nice ladies doing a good deed."

Ann Marie Eidenbach's face was pointed away from Ashley, so the receptionist didn't see the change in her eyes and her expression.

Janet did, and when Debbie hummed lightly, Janet knew she'd seen it too.

"May I send them over? Or should I send them packing?" Ashley posed the question lightly. "Your choice, Miss Eidenbach."

The woman glared at Ashley and then at Janet and Debbie. Then she deliberately averted her gaze. "Nothing of mine left in that old place, I can guarantee you that. That's all I've got to say about it. Leave me alone."

Ashley straightened. "Yes ma'am." She came back to Janet and Debbie with a regretful expression. "Sorry, ladies." She ushered them back in the direction of the reception area. "She doesn't care to be seen at the moment."

"I got that." Janet kept her expression compassionate but angled herself so that she could pay attention to Ashley but still see Ann Marie. Feigning nonchalance, she withdrew the packet of letters from her tote bag and made sure to hold it where Ann Marie would be able to see it.

Janet was confident her ploy had worked when the elderly woman's brows knit even more firmly.

"Ashley, if she changes her mind, can you give us a call? I've included my cell phone number on here." She handed Ashley one of their business cards and tucked the ribbon-tied packet back into her bag. "Thanks for trying."

"Always happy to help," Ashley replied as she returned to her desk. "And thank you again for the cookies. I'll see that Ray and

Eileen get theirs when the movie wraps up. And her too." She gestured to Ann Marie across the way. "Won't they all be surprised?"

"Thanks, Ashley," Janet told her. "Have a good one."

"You too."

Debbie waited until they were in the car then blurted, "Miss Eidenbach knows something."

"She looked quite angry when I pulled those letters out of my bag," Janet agreed.

"But why?" Debbie mused as Janet started the engine. "If they're not hers, why put up a fuss about seeing us? Unless she was the one redacting the pertinent information."

"Did you see the expression she aimed at us? Like she was caught and trying to figure how to get herself out of the snare. Maybe if we give it a little time, she'll come around. Maybe." Janet placed her chilled hands over the warm vents. "Time to dig out the gloves."

"And hats."

"I hate hat hair."

"So does every woman I know, but if you live up here, you deal with it."

"Unless you're in high school," Janet lamented. "It wasn't until some of Tiffany's favorite singers started sporting winter hats that she'd even consider putting one on. It was a choose-your-battles kind of time, and the hat wasn't worth the argument. On top of that, she didn't get one bit sick, so I didn't even have that leg to stand on."

"Julian always wears a hat when it's close to freezing, but Jaxon never does. Same reason."

"Kids." Janet laughed.

"Yep. Reminds me of two best friends who never wore hats and shared makeup, even though we weren't supposed to because my mother was a total germaphobe."

"If that was the worst we did, our parents got off easy," Janet said as she pulled into Debbie's driveway. "See you tomorrow."

"Will do." Debbie dashed into the house. Janet pulled away as Greg's pickup truck turned into the driveway.

She waved to him, and he waved back as he climbed out and then hurried toward the front door.

Janet caught a glimpse of her best friend greeting Greg with a hug and a kiss before she got past the deciduous bushes separating Debbie's house from her next-door neighbor's place.

She loved seeing Debbie happy, and the unanticipated romance was truly icing on the cake. If that embrace meant anything, she'd better get that cookbook done soon.

She was parking her car at home when Jim Watson called. She answered, still in the driver's seat.

"Hey, Jim. What's up?"

"My quest to coax more Palmers home is meeting with multiple snags," he admitted, sounding genuinely disappointed. "I was hoping to have better results, and it's getting late for anyone to book a flight now if they need to fly. You know what road travel in winter weather is like."

"All we can do is try, Jim. And pray. Kim may have bitten off more than she realized with this idea, despite her wonderful intentions."

"I agree. I'm not quite ready to give up yet. Also, I thought I'd mention something—Troy Henry stopped by to see me an hour or so ago. Now, he's not normally a barrel of laughs under the best circumstances, but he said someone is trying to outmaneuver him in a real estate sale on the outskirts of town. A plot of land that's supposed to be coming up for sale between Good Shepherd, the old stone church property, and Claymont Creek Farm."

Janet had reached for the door handle to let herself out of the car, but she froze at Jim's words. "Someone is trying to buy land over there? Did he say who?"

"He didn't," Jim reported. "You know Troy. I'm pretty sure he didn't want me to jump into the fray and become a third player. I'm not interested in buying property, but I wouldn't be surprised to see that side of town develop into a more suburban-style setting. We've got such a nice reputation here, and people are eager to get out of cities. The way our population is increasing now is indicative of something, isn't it?"

"Sure is. Was Troy really upset? He's not used to being outbid or having things yanked out from under him. He doesn't generally buy vacant land, but he's got a good nose for real estate investment, that's for sure."

"You've got that right. He said it's not a done deal, but he's poking around to see who's courting whom, if you get my drift. You know whose farm lies in the center of that particular triangle?"

She sure did. "Charlie Briscoe's."

"And if there was ever someone who knew how to hold out for the highest bidder, it's Charlie. He's had brains from the get-go. Troy's thinking that maybe Charlie didn't come home to run the farm after all. That maybe he bought it as an investment because he had information about those planned manufacturing sites in New Philadelphia."

That was a new avenue of thought. "So maybe he's in the market for speculation?"

"It's a lot easier to make money on real estate investments when you have an idea about what's going on and where. Charlie's firm in Chicago handles the bank for one of those manufacturers. I'm not saying he's acting on insider information, but…" Jim let the words trail off.

"But a wise man puts his money where it will make the most return." Was this what Rick and Charlie were discussing the other day? Their heated expressions had indicated that it was a less-than-friendly conversation. Rick had stated to Janet and Debbie that he saw Claymont Creek Farm as an asset to development the way it was. Maybe Charlie felt differently, and his car had been seen near the farm, according to Dani's neighbor. Or had Rick and Charlie simply clashed because they both wanted to develop on the Briscoe family land?

"I need to let you go, Janet. I have deadlines." True to form, Jim stayed matter-of-fact. It was one of the reasons people trusted him for advice. "I just wanted to update you on my progress with Kim's brothers, and I knew you'd be interested in Troy's take on the real estate market. What with the odd things going on at the Addison farm right now."

Janet wasn't sure if she liked the Claymont Creek Farm information being common knowledge, but there was nothing she could do about that. "Strange stuff, Jim."

"I'll say. No one should be pestering a fine family like the Addisons. Clint is known for his grudge-holding capabilities, but Agnes and the kids are wonderful. Plus Clint's mellowed a good bit as he's gotten older."

That assertion puzzled Janet. "Has he?"

"Absolutely." Jim sounded certain. "After that scare with their granddaughter, he turned a new leaf. I've seen it numerous times. He's the first in line to help when there's trouble, whether it's from fire or illness or anything else. Quietly, of course. He's not one to want anyone else to see or mention it. He saw how the community rallied around Kelsey, and I think it made him see things in a new light. A welcome one at that."

"That's good to know. Thanks for everything, Jim."

"Sure thing. Talk to you later." He disconnected, but his comment continued to puzzle her.

Clint Addison was quick to help others.

He'd been a solid help to his son and daughter-in-law when Kelsey was being treated for leukemia.

But he didn't pay Dean now. Did he assume he'd paid it forward back then? Had his help been so extensive that he figured Dean owed him? But that didn't fit with Jim's assessment of Clint's generosity, and Dean was his son.

"What do you do when you've got too many puzzle pieces and not enough space in the puzzle?" she asked Ian when he got home half an hour later.

He took the strange conversation starter in stride. "You consider that maybe you've got more than one puzzle in the box."

Of course.

"Remember that puzzle we worked on three years ago, and you were about to throw the whole thing away?" he asked.

"But I didn't. I practiced restraint," she reminded him with a laugh as she started the pasta. "It was insanely frustrating because it had pieces from that other fall puzzle in the box." One of Tiffany's friends had spilled another puzzle box onto the table. She'd cleaned it up as best she could, but the extra pieces had wrought havoc in Janet's brain before she realized that at least three dozen pieces on the table weren't meant for that puzzle. "So maybe I'm looking at multiple questions and trying to make the answers fit the wrong one."

"Keep it simple."

He was right. She'd been layering her ideas into could-have-beens, and that might be confusing the issues. "Good advice. Are you still meeting up with Greg and the boys tonight?"

"We're doing a skills workout at the middle school gym with Julian, Jaxon, and a few of their friends, but we can't start until after eight. That's when the school practices are done." He opened a jar of marinara sauce Janet had canned with home-grown vegetables over the summer. "I told Julian I'd go over some offensive strategies with him for basketball. The kid's got moves. You know kids. Their dad can tell them something and they shrug it off, but if I say the exact same thing, they're like 'Wow, Chief. That works.'"

"Another adult always knows more than your own mom or dad."

He grinned. "Yep. And I saw your recipe layout on the table, which means you're working on the cookbook tonight."

"The holidays take a big bite of time, and if I want to get it into production, I have to get it done," she told him. "I'd like to have it ready by spring."

He leaned over and gave her a kiss. "I have no doubts that you'll make it, love. None at all. How's that rigatoni coming?"

"Two minutes, and that goes for the meatballs as well."

"Great. How'd everything go at Good Shepherd? Were you there to see Ray? Or Eileen?"

"Neither. Ann Marie Eidenbach."

He frowned. "I have no idea who that is."

"A rather crotchety old woman who knows something about a packet of old letters that was found in one of Red Meyers's properties."

"How did you find a packet of letters from one of Red's houses?"

"I didn't. Red's family donated a box of war memorabilia to the museum, and the letters were in it. It should have been an easy trace but the names and addresses on the envelopes were all redacted. The letters inside were all sent to 'my dearest wife' and signed by 'your loving husband.' So we have absolutely nothing to go on."

"It's a federal offense to tamper with US mail," Ian said in a stern tone she knew all too well.

Janet poured the rigatoni noodles into a colander in the sink. "I suppose it is."

"Serious enough to have multiple codes covering it," he said. "It's considered a major offense because people trust the United States Postal Service to get things where they belong. Misdirecting mail is a crime."

Janet left the pasta to drain and got the packet of letters from her bag to show Ian. "To be fair, we don't know if they were tampered with before being received or after. This is what I'm working with."

He took the packet and whistled softly. "Someone didn't want these names and addresses to get out."

"Yup."

"But I might have an answer for you."

Now, that was an interesting and unexpected reply. "How?"

"We might be able to scan the envelopes and read the content behind the ink. It doesn't always work, depending on how well they hid the information. If they used a blocking device like paste before the marker, the extra whitening layer makes it unreadable. But that probably wasn't even known back then because no one was scanning anything."

"Can we try it?"

"I'll take one to the office tomorrow. Our scanner isn't top of the line or anything, but it gets the job done. I'll have to cut the envelope open to get it to lie flat on the screen."

She cringed, but agreed. "We can always glue or tape it back together."

"Sure. It might give us some answers and save you gals some legwork. But the question with these isn't just who blacked them out," he went on. "It's why? What did they hope to gain, or what were they hiding?"

Janet had been asking herself the same question. "A romance her parents wouldn't approve of would be my guess. The letters are very loving, and there's no way to know whether the soldier who wrote them made it home or not without his identity."

"If we can read the name or the address, that will narrow things down for you." He set the packet down. "But for now, let's eat."

# CHAPTER TWELVE

Ian called Janet shortly before closing time the following after-noon. "There was very little we could see with the scan, love. A few numbers on the soldier's side, and three faint letters on the addressee's. The letters were at various spots, not together. We did see part of the word 'Dennison,' though, so that means that at least this letter came through our local post office."

"So we know the letters came here."

"Assuming the others all have Dennison in the last line, yes."

"And we know Ann Marie was a letter sorter at the local level," Janet mused. "They were found inside the house she rented for nearly thirty years after her parents died. She never married, accord-ing to Lettie Karras. I double-checked the county records, which seem to confirm that."

"Indicative but still circumstantial," he told her. "Someone else may have boarded there over the years. She would have had extra space after her parents died. It wouldn't have been unusual for someone to rent out a room to bring in extra money. How old is Ann Marie?"

"In her eighties."

"We might want to be careful about accusing an old lady in a nursing facility of a crime. I'm not sure of the statute of limitations on something like this off the top of my head, but I'm going to guess that it's less than sixty years."

"I wasn't even thinking of legal ramifications," Janet assured him. "But that doesn't mean we can't find a way to get the letters where they belong."

"If that person or place still exists. I'll stop by in a bit to bring it back to you."

He was being sensible, but Janet wasn't interested in the sensible side of this situation. She wanted the romantic side, a husband's words going awry. Unless he was Ann Marie's husband, and they'd been married in a different county, or perhaps even under different names.

She posed the idea to Debbie while they finished cleaning.

Debbie considered it. "I think Ann Marie would be more interested in the letters if that were the case. Maybe upset about the fate of her beloved, but she'd still want the letters, wouldn't she? I kept Reed's letters after he was killed."

It was a valid point, but Ian walked in before Janet could think on it. He held the envelope in one hand and a notepad in the other. "Here you go. I wish it was more."

He'd recorded the information from the scanner on the notepad. The random numbers from the return address meant nothing to the women. An old soldier like Ray might make some sense of them, but it was the letters they discerned above the word Dennison that Janet wanted to see.

"We saw a lowercase *i* in the first word and maybe the upstroke of an *f* in that word too. There could have been an *a* in the second word. The handwriting isn't great," he explained. "Kind of crunched and curled together, maybe written quickly. I can try the other envelopes and see if we can see anything else. That might help."

"It would. The more we have, the easier it will be to piece it together," Debbie said. "By the way, thank you for taking the time to work with the boys last night. Greg says you're a born coach and that all the boys listened to you and took your words to heart."

"I think that's got more to do with me being a cop rather than my basketball prowess, but I'll take it." Ian grinned. "I need to get over to Uhrichsville. We wanted to have an in-person chat about what's going on around Claymont Creek Farm. It's out of their jurisdiction, but it's always good to work together."

"Part of what makes you so good at your job," Janet said proudly. "See you tonight. Leftover pasta and burgers."

He chuckled. "Works for me. I'll be home tonight. That's a nice thought."

They were home together until Ian was called out to a motor vehicle accident shortly after eight. He gave Janet a quick hug before hurrying to his cruiser. He called her half an hour later. "It's Hailey Adams, the animal activist. I don't think she's seriously hurt, but she says she was run off the road by a dark vehicle. They're taking her to the ER to be safe. The car's a mess, probably totaled. She's in a state, understandably."

"How scary for her."

"Absolutely."

Dani's neighbor Mack had seen a dark vehicle parked near the Addison farm several times. He'd identified it as Charlie Briscoe's car.

Then, Charlie had been at Rick Radner's development company, having words with Rick about something. He had been driving a big, dark car. Not to mention the dark SUV that had parked at her own home, though she couldn't say for sure whether Charlie had been at the wheel.

"Ian, how likely is it that a big, dark vehicle keeps turning up?"

"Janet, everyone and their brother has a big, dark vehicle. Check any parking lot in town. Every one of them is filled with black and dark gray vehicles, especially if you're talking SUVs. I fight a headache whenever a witness says the words 'Dark vehicle. Black or dark gray.' Without a plate number, it's like a needle in a haystack." He paused, then asked, "You wouldn't happen to have a particular driver in mind, would you?"

"Not with evidence behind it," she admitted.

"Okay, what name do you have with no evidence?"

"Charlie Briscoe," she said quietly.

"I see. Charlie might drive a big, dark SUV, but so do literally hundreds of other people around here. And why would a well-off guy like Charlie want to mess with someone like Hailey?"

"I have no idea, but he's been seen around the fringes of this thing for a while. Perhaps she's drawing negative attention to the farm or to the area in general." The moment she voiced the thought, she saw holes in the theory. Why would anyone risk all he'd accomplished over the years to mess with an annoyance? "You're right, it doesn't add up. But there's something going on between Charlie and Rick. I saw that myself. It wasn't a casual conversation. Where did the accident happen?"

"Near the tree farm."

The tree farm was situated north of the Addisons' spread.

"Hailey was heading north," he continued. "The other driver was heading south. He or she crossed lanes, and Hailey steered off the road to avoid a possible head-on collision, at least according to her. This could simply be a case of distracted driving, texting or something. In any case, there were no witnesses, and she saw very little because she was trying to keep her car out of the ditch. Unfortunately, that's where she ended up anyway. I'm pulling into the ER parking lot right now. I'll be late tonight and try not to wake you, but I'll come by for coffee in the morning, all right?"

"Yes. Be safe, Ian."

"Will do, and right back at you. Love you."

Janet added this latest item to her already convoluted list of thoughts on Dani's problems.

Her list grew the following morning. She'd poured Harry his first cup of coffee when Dani's call came through shortly after seven. "Janet, our chickens were set free last night."

"Oh no." Was that why Hailey was driving on their road? Had she been there to free Agnes's pet hens?

The Addisons didn't use chickens for egg production or even for meat. Agnes kept her small flock like some people kept a cat or a dog. She loved her birds, and Clint had set up a cute enclosure for them so people could visit the nine birds that called the upscale chicken coop home.

Agnes even used the chicken area as an annual fundraiser event for various local charities. According to a report Jim Watson had done the week before, the "chicken buckets," designed to resemble a bucket of chicken from fried chicken restaurants, had already collected nearly a thousand dollars for the local food pantries. Had the buckets spurred Hailey's actions? Or was it the thought of caged chickens that brought out her ire? Janet wasn't sure, but she intended to track Hailey down and ask as soon as she could.

"We've recovered six, but three have disappeared. Mom is distraught. We're hoping they'll come home at dusk because that's their natural instinct." Dani sighed. "What on earth is going on around here?"

Janet couldn't mention Hailey. It wasn't confidential information, but she wasn't about to spread conjecture about what happened to the chickens, because she didn't truly know. She might *suspect* Hailey, but circumstantial evidence was often wrong or misinterpreted. Years of being married to a cop had taught her to avoid assumptions. Or at least that Ian wanted her to avoid assumptions.

"I don't know, but can we stop by later this afternoon?" Janet asked. "I know you're busy with orders for the fried cake fundraisers."

"That should be fine. Those fundraiser profits keep us afloat during the quieter weeks of early November. Once we get to the end of the month, the holidays and parties and desserts do the rest. Dad was skeptical when I came up with the idea, but he's definitely seen the light in the past few years, when we've cleared thousands in those few weeks. It's become a major fundraising activity throughout the area. Speaking of which, the van is here to pick up today's orders."

Her words haunted Janet's thoughts all morning. When things quieted down after lunch, she posed a question to Debbie. "Could someone be targeting the Addisons because of their successful fried cake fundraisers?"

Debbie stared at her in confusion.

"Okay, it's a strange question," Janet admitted. "I get how it would be weird to target a place or a company because they're helping local nonprofits raise money, but hear me out. What if their success became someone else's undoing? Dani's fried cake business has taken over a major market share of fall fundraising for a large sector of southeast Ohio. It begins in late October and goes through the third week of November. That effort alone generates thousands in profit. Maybe another business has lost a lot of customers to Dani's fried cakes. It seems like every school, team, church, hospital, and other kind of group has autumn fundraisers."

Debbie wiped down the dishwashing area as the last load went in. "I had no idea that using fried cakes for fundraisers was a thing. I know the boys sold the fried cakes two weeks ago for the football team, but it didn't occur to me it was anything more than something local. No one was allowed to sell things at the firm in Cleveland, even if it was for a nonprofit or a good cause." She put the dishcloth in the laundry basket. "I would get plenty of personal holiday requests to help the food pantries and shelters for Thanksgiving, but I wouldn't have known that fried cakes were a big deal."

"That's a huge fundraiser here." Janet finished sealing her frosting containers and stored them. Paulette had gone home a few minutes before, and they were ready to head to New Philadelphia to see Hailey. "I didn't realize how big until Dani tossed that profit margin into the conversation. Cutting that far into another company's earning potential could make the Addisons a potential target."

"What are some of the other fundraisers around here?" asked Debbie.

"Candy bars, off the top of my head. Not that I think the CEO of some big candy company is trying to sabotage them, but what about the other farms that grow chrysanthemums for fundraisers? Or maybe there were other bakeries that did similar things, and the organizations chose the Addisons instead? If the cakes are amazing and you make a clear profit while someone else is doing all the work, I can see why that would be an attractive fundraising campaign."

"Now that's a possibility." Debbie shut off the lights and locked the door behind them. "We could ask about it when we see Dani, because she'd most likely know if they got contracts that used to be awarded to someone else. Did the Third Street Bakery ever do that sort of thing?"

Janet shook her head as she climbed into the passenger seat of Debbie's car. "They never got into that side of marketing. I honestly don't think it would have occurred to them. They were older and doing perfectly fine without expansion."

"So using the fried cakes for a fundraiser is a relatively new thing."

"That's right. Hey, are we running by the place where Hailey went off the road?"

"We sure are," Debbie confirmed. "It will take a little longer to get to Hailey's place this way, but I'd like to see exactly where it happened."

Janet couldn't have said it better herself. She didn't know what clues they might pick up after the police had already been over the area. But with the Addisons' saboteur ramping up the seriousness of his or her activities, they couldn't leave a single stone unturned.

# CHAPTER THIRTEEN

There was little to see when they got to the section of road that Ian had indicated. They passed Mack's pretty house and yard and then Claymont Creek Farm. Charlie's farm was on the next road east of them and an easy drive into the village. Either property would make a good target for development. Would Charlie see the Addisons' farm as a competitor for a land bid? Would he make his uncle's old adversary look bad to win a sales contract for the Briscoe acreage?

Debbie pulled off the road about a quarter mile past the Addisons' donkey pull area and pointed toward the ditch. "This should be it. Fresh digs in the side as if someone nose-dived into the ditch and couldn't get wheel traction to back out."

"You can see where she swerved right here." Janet pointed to tire marks leading from the northbound lane to the narrow shoulder of the road. "So was it coincidental that she was right here the same evening the Addison chickens were released from their pen?"

Debbie grimaced. "Doesn't seem likely, does it? But unless there are chicken feathers in her car—"

Janet hadn't thought of that. "That would be an awesome find."

Debbie appeared skeptical. "Even that wouldn't be proof unless they sent it out for chicken DNA, which sounds unlikely. You ready to talk to her in person?"

"If she'll see us," Janet said.

They pulled into Hailey's driveway fifteen minutes later. The modular home was set a short distance off the road, and it was in rough shape. Modular homes weren't uncommon in the rural areas connecting the small towns of southeast Ohio. They offered affordable housing and independent living, but this one had fallen into disrepair and stayed there.

They approached the door.

"No dog? Or just no dog that barks at strangers?" Janet whispered as they drew closer. "I expected at least one dog, plus a zoo's worth of cats, turtles, and mice. Anything that might need saving."

Debbie scanned their surroundings. "Apparently your expectations were off the mark."

Janet knocked on the door. No one answered, so she tried again. Still nothing. They could either go home unsatisfied, or—

Janet called the number she'd programmed into her phone the night before.

Debbie arched a brow in surprise. "You have her number?"

"I did a web search after Ian was called out for her accident."

To Janet's surprise, Hailey answered the call. "Hello?"

"Hailey, this is Janet Shaw from the Whistle Stop Café in Dennison. I heard you had a bit of trouble yesterday, and I wanted to drop off some cookies. My husband was one of the policemen you met last night. I'm outside your door with my friend Debbie. We own the café together. Should I leave the cookies here, on the bench?"

A small red wooden bench sat somewhat crookedly in a stony area outside the trailer's door.

"Stay put. I'm coming."

Janet shot Debbie a satisfied expression, but it disappeared when Hailey opened her door.

The woman looked terrible. Red-rimmed, swollen eyes indicated she'd been crying. Her face was scraped, her left eye was blackened, and her arm was in a sling.

"Oh, Hailey. I'm so sorry." She meant it too. She hadn't realized that "minor injuries" would be so bad.

"Thank you. The airbag saved me from worse injuries, no doubt, but the way the car landed made it impossible for me to get out because there wasn't enough clearance for me to open the driver's side door. The passenger door was jammed against a tree root. Once I realized I was trapped, I was glad I'd decided to use the last of my savings to fix my phone. How long would it have taken someone to find me if I hadn't been able to call 911? It's not like that road is on a regular patrol route."

She was right. The quiet road didn't garner a lot of law enforcement attention, because it wasn't widely traveled at night. But it was the comment about her phone that caught Janet's attention. Tight funds and a wrecked car were a nightmare situation.

"Hi, Hailey. I'm Debbie Albright," Debbie said. "We saw you at Claymont Creek Farm a couple of weeks back. You were angry about something." Debbie left the comment open, not pushing, but Hailey glared at her nonetheless.

"Those poor little donkeys." She hugged herself with her free arm. It was cold out, but she didn't ask them to step in. "They're precious, and those people are using them for profit, profit, and more profit. I stop and give them treats all winter long. Did you know that they leave them out there, in that shed, with nothing but hay to eat?"

Her distressed expression made it clear that she thought the Addisons were negligent donkey owners, but Janet knew differently. Dani was careful about their diet and worked with a horse veterinarian up in Walnut Creek to take care of her herd and keep them in peak health.

"Everyone knows that they need grain to build up their resistance to cold. And it gets really cold out there," Hailey went on. "I'm not oblivious to their choices and how they misuse those poor animals."

"And the chickens?" Janet posed the question lightly.

Hailey frowned. "They're chickens."

"But they're outside all year."

Hailey waved that off. "Birds adapt to conditions rapidly. They're used to being outside, and the Addisons built them a fancy house to live in. It might be bigger than mine. I don't begrudge them, though. The chickens, that is. It's good for them to live the high life. They don't live long, you see."

Janet had never thought about that, but she nodded.

"Whereas the miniature donkeys can live for twenty-five or thirty years. Pulling carts, living in the bitter cold in an uninsulated open shed—well, that's abuse, plain and simple. Why should a donkey have to pull a cart all day long? Not be able to lie down when they're tired?"

Debbie offered the practical side of farm life. "I suppose having each exhibit pull its own weight is part of what makes a farm successful."

"A donkey isn't an 'exhibit.' It's a living creature, with feelings and a will of its own."

"Bad choice of words on my part," Debbie said, backpedaling. "But the essence is the same, isn't it? Using animals in their normal capacity is conducive to farming."

"But they're not being used in their normal capacity," Hailey shot back. "There's nothing normal about making a donkey pull children around a trail." Her cheeks were pink, and her brows knit tightly. "We live in an area where people are forcing God's creatures to do unnatural things all the time. Cows having babies every year, and then having those babies taken away from them shortly after birth. Donkeys pulling carts. Horses racing or pulling big heavy plows. It's reprehensible, I tell you."

Janet held out the small box of cookies, confident she had the answer she needed. "Here. I don't want you to freeze out here, and we wanted you to know that we were sorry about the accident. Was the other car familiar at all?"

Hailey accepted the cookies. "I can't say for sure, but I saw Charlie Briscoe on that road earlier. Right after dark. I was driving to Dennison because I had an appointment there. I can't say it was him who ran me off the road, but the car was very similar. It's not like I'm memorizing license plate numbers on other cars while I'm driving."

"Of course not," Janet said. "It probably happened too fast to see much."

"Between the darkness and the headlights glaring, I was practically blinded. They were those new bright-white LED ones. Ridiculous to even allow such things on the road." She took another step back. "I need to go in. I'm cold."

"Of course. Please take care of yourself."

"Thank you. And thanks for the cookies."

The door shut firmly behind her.

Janet and Debbie crossed the yard to Debbie's car. They didn't say a word until they were in the car and moving down the road. Debbie pulled off to the side in a little strip mall and indicated the coffee shop at the far end. "I'm buying. We need to talk before we get to Dani's."

They grabbed coffees and brought them back to the car.

"I don't think she had anything to do with the chickens last night," Janet announced.

"I agree." Debbie frowned. "I was watching her carefully, but there was no reaction when you brought it up. She didn't seem to be against anything the Addisons are doing with their chickens, even though she had plenty to say about the donkeys."

Janet couldn't disagree. "But what about her seeing Charlie?"

"Personally, I wonder how she even knows him. Does Charlie own animals?"

Janet shrugged. "I have no idea."

"Hailey didn't go to school with us."

"No, she's several years younger. But Charlie's name was all over the papers back then. And the villages here are quite small. If you live here long enough, there aren't a lot of people you don't know."

Debbie lifted her coffee cup in salute. "Another major difference from the city."

"That's right. Let's go talk to Dani. I want to see if she knows how often Charlie makes a run up and down that road and if he's approached them about selling the farm. Maybe he's trying to make a bigger land deal than we imagined."

They pulled into Claymont Creek Farm's parking lot in no time. Dusk elongated the shadows of the spruce grove bordering the western side of the sales areas. The mix of spruces provided an organic backdrop for the seasonal displays. Beyond the trees lay seventy acres of orchard and farmland. The Addisons rented additional acreage north of Mack's house up the road, and Janet had seen Clint working Mack's acreage in the past. Development and agriculture bumped heads in a lot of places, but that hadn't been a problem here because the towns hadn't seen growth in a long time. That seemed to be changing now. It remained to be seen what that change would bring.

Dani met them by the sales barn. "I want our conversation to be private," she told them as they moved inside to the pristine kitchen. "Mom's trying to keep Dad from worrying, and Dad's trying not to worry, which just makes him worry more. It all leaves me spinning plates."

"Plates that are usually spun by three of you," Janet said. "It's hard to suddenly become a crew of one to oversee everything."

Dani waved that away. "This is actually the best time of year for that. Everything is out of the fields and up here, waiting to be sold. The outdoor displays are cleaned up and packed away because shopping outdoors in a cold drizzle isn't nearly as inviting as coming in here, smelling so many good things and grabbing holiday treats. Other than the Living Nativity in December, all we do now is bake up a storm, make a gazillion fried cakes, and run the retail side of things."

"That in itself is pretty impressive," Debbie pointed out.

Dani leaned back against the bakery display counter. "It's more manageable than it sounds—with help, of course. It's doable because it's all here in a central location. If this had happened in August or

September, I'd be in a state of frenzy. Plus, I've got some good friends who have been helping out. That's a blessing."

"That's good to know. I was concerned about how you were going to manage everything," Janet said. "I'm glad it's working out so far."

"It's going as well as I could hope for." Dani lifted a small plate of apple-pie cookies and held it out to them.

As Janet and Debbie each took one, Debbie told her friend, "Now please hide the tray because these are one of my favorites."

"Janet's recipe. She's never been afraid to coach me or share things with me," Dani said as she slid the tray out of sight. She smiled at Janet then shifted gears back to the farm. "Mack called me earlier. He said that a car went into the ditch up the road last night. He saw the flashing lights and headed down to check things out. He said it was that animal activist in the ditch. I expect she was hurrying away from here after she sneaked through the display area and released Mom's birds."

"I don't think she did it," Janet said.

Dani gave her a skeptical expression.

"We just came from dropping off cookies for her," Debbie explained. "We wanted to see if she would offer up anything intentionally or unintentionally to give us a clue, but she didn't. In fact, she seems to respect your fancy chicken house because it keeps the chickens safe."

"She's right about that," Dani said with pride. "Every carnivorous creature in the area tries to figure out a way to bag a free chicken dinner. Fox, skunks, weasels, dogs. Not Rusty," she added, referring to their trusty yellow Lab. "He learned to leave the chickens alone when he was young, and he does a good job of warning us about people coming by the house."

"Did the trail cameras show anything?" asked Janet.

Dani crossed her arms over her chest. "None of them point at the chicken yard directly, but the ones at the donkey area catch a bit of that sector. Not enough to make out anything. Honestly, you could come in low, poke up the latch on the chicken pen, and be out of there in seconds. None of the cameras would catch that."

"Charlie Briscoe's car might have been seen on the road last night. You're sure he's not carrying on that silly old feud between his uncle and your father?"

Dani gaped at her. "Why would Charlie want to mess up another farmer's place? Or livelihood? What made you think that? You girls went to school with Charlie, same as me. He's one of the good guys."

"He was, for sure, but that was over twenty years ago," Janet pointed out. "People change. If there's a land deal in the works or people are hedging their bets on other people's land or prospects, that might be right up Charlie's alley. I know there was bad blood between his family and yours."

Dani shrugged that off. "Two overzealous farmers who always had to be right. My dad has calmed down over the last dozen years, and Mitchell Briscoe is out of the picture now. Charlie would never do anything to hurt anyone."

Janet wasn't sure how far to push the issue, so she was grateful when Debbie added an important piece of information to the conversation. "His car's been seen in the area several times according to your neighbor."

Dani raised an eyebrow. "Mack said that?"

Janet nodded. "He mentioned it when the ovens weren't working and we drove up that way. Speaking of, his farm truly is lovely. I remember when that back field, the one you guys rent from him now, was all orchards. Of course, setting an orchard has changed a lot in the last twenty years. It's like a whole new level of science, isn't it?"

"Orcharding has become more of an art form," Dani replied. "And it's extremely expensive to get into. Very different from when we helped Mack remove his trees because of that nasty root fungus that spread throughout his soil. Avoiding disease in the orchards is so much easier than treating it once it's taken hold. Mack wanted to replant his, but the fungus can live in the soil for years, and no one wants to burn money carelessly."

"What a shame," Debbie murmured.

"It was. Fortunately, we've learned a lot in the last couple of decades," Dani said. "Dad is reluctant to change things, but I want to try out some of the new, smaller trees when we need to replant. Maybe even use espalier fencing to train the branches out. Open branches and sun help keep the trees healthy. Healthy trees give a better yield. But like I said, replanting comes with an expensive price tag attached. I'm keeping that to myself for now because it's bound to cause an argument, and I don't want to rile Dad up right now."

"You know your stuff."

Dani gave a wry smile. "I've made enough mistakes to teach me a thing or two."

"It was the same way with baking for me," Janet said. "I taught myself, learned as much as I could at the Third Street Bakery, and then kept learning by trial and error."

"Well, I appreciate you passing your wisdom on to me, and I'll happily return the favor if I can," Dani told her.

"I may take you up on that." Janet checked her watch. "We'd better be on our way. I have an online meeting with the people in charge of the Light Up the Town event. It's coming up quick, and Debbie and I are running a cookie-and-hot cocoa booth outside the depot. We also scored a booth at the Christkindl Market next weekend."

Dani started walking them toward the door. "We'll be at Christkindl too. It's such a great way to get our products into the town, and people love to shop the marketplace venues. Dad thought we were taking on too much, but Amelia and Kelsey volunteered to run the booth. I also wrangled a space for Light Up the Town."

"That's wonderful," Debbie said. "The more the merrier."

"We're doing fudge samples there. I was over the moon when they approved my application. I wasn't sure they would since the farm is technically outside the village borders, but they did."

"That event is a great kickoff to the holiday season," Debbie said. "We'll have the Nativity in the gazebo and the big tree set up across from the bank. And lights and displays here, there, and everywhere. It's wonderful."

"The whole thing is marvelous," Janet agreed. "And the committee has told me that the entire event was funded by an anonymous donor. Several people on the committee have guessed it was Rick Radner, but no one's sure. He's been doing a lot to improve Dennison, and his efforts have inspired others to do the same."

"Well, it's very nice of him to do it, if it was him. Although if he wants to remain anonymous, I respect that. Not everything needs to be lauded in the court of public opinion." Dani locked the barn's double glass doors when they got outside. "Is Hailey going to be all right? I never asked."

"She's pretty banged up from the airbag onslaught, but yes," Janet assured her. "She has plenty of bumps and bruises, plus one arm in a sling. She should be fine in a few weeks. On the other hand, her car was totaled, and I don't think she has the funds to get a new one. Especially since her old one wasn't worth much. Collision insurance is pricey when you're counting pennies."

"Is she struggling financially?" Dani asked.

"We don't exactly have access to her financial records, but going by what we saw today, I'd say so," Debbie said.

"Oh dear. I didn't know that." Concern deepened the lines between Dani's brows. "She always looks fine when she shows up at events. Except now that you mention it, it's usually the exact same outfit—blue jeans and a T-shirt or a sweater and that trench coat. Not like that's unusual. The trench coat is a name brand."

"And could have been gotten as a gift or in a thrift shop," Janet said. "Everyone is thrifting these days. It's a great way to get the most use out of something. We'll keep you posted if we hear anything, okay?"

"Yes. Thank you for dropping by, and for everything else. I mean that sincerely," Dani added. "I so appreciate your efforts."

They were kind words, offered genuinely, but when the two got into the car, Janet exchanged a look with Debbie. "Except what have we got, my friend? Not much."

Debbie disagreed as she backed out of the parking space. "We've ruled people out, like Rick and likely Hailey. I say we have a little chat with Charlie Briscoe ourselves. The Charlie we knew in school was a great guy, but he was also incredibly competitive. That works on the football field, and it obviously worked for him in business. We should see if that competitive edge is guiding his actions here."

"Agreed. Let's aim for Monday," Janet suggested. "Hey, do you and Greg and the boys want to join us for brisket and football on Sunday? Ian is going to fire up the smoker, and you know he makes the best brisket around."

"I would, but I'm having Paulette and Greg and the boys over for Sunday dinner, kind of a precursor to hosting Thanksgiving at my place with both Paulette and my parents there. Which shouldn't be a big deal, right? It's Sunday and football, and it should just be five people who like each other getting together. Yet I'm insanely nervous about it, for some reason. It makes no sense, because it's not like the first time they've been there."

"It makes perfect sense," Janet assured her. "You're stepping into a new normal. Of course you're nervous. Anyone would be because kids change everything. That's okay. You're great with those boys. When you had that heart-to-heart with Jaxon a few weeks ago, you gave him the freedom to hang on to the past and step into the future. If Paulette's right—"

"And she usually is," Debbie said with a laugh.

"The boys like you, at least eighty percent of the time," Janet said, grinning so her friend knew she was teasing. "That's amazing because most parents of teens are in the doghouse at least seventy-five percent of the time. You're already ahead of the curve."

"I want them to feel at home. Not just with me but with my house. With everything." Debbie rounded the corner onto Janet's street. "I keep researching online about blending families. I also talked with Pastor Nick, and he was simply wonderful. Very reassuring. But then I have to bite my tongue if one of the boys gives Greg a hard time. I'm not used to taking a back seat."

"Then don't think of it as a back seat," Janet advised as Debbie parked in the driveway. "Think of it as a supporting role. That's where your wisdom comes into play, your flair for timing. Kids will always go toe to toe with parents, like we did. Like Tiffany did. It's the quiet guidance after things cool off that helps direct their path."

"That makes so much sense, Janet. Thank you."

Janet winked. "Not my first rodeo. And I haven't missed your mother's unbridled excitement about what the future might hold. She's almost giddy. But that probably puts more pressure on you, doesn't it?"

Debbie nodded. "I'm not the typical twentysomething who can't wait to be a bride. There's a big difference between approaching the thought of marriage now and back then, but I know she's got two bridal magazines tucked away. She stuffed them into the recipe drawer when I stopped by a few days ago." She closed her eyes briefly. "I think a part of her has been waiting for something like this for twenty years. Now it could be real because I honestly can't imagine not spending the rest of my life with Greg. I think he feels the same way about me. I hope he does, anyway."

Janet patted her hand, certain Greg did feel that way. "Take it day by day. Make a plan, but be prepared to adjust it as you go. That's how it is with kids and extended family. Things happen, so we have to stay flexible. But honestly, I can't think of anyone better suited to handle this than you, Debbie. I mean that sincerely."

"I know you do." Debbie beamed. "I'll see you in the morning. I'm staying late tomorrow to do the deep cleaning. Do you want to try seeing Ann Marie on your own? She might be more comfortable with just one of us coming by."

"I'll give it a shot," Janet told her as she opened the door. "Depending on her mood, scrubbing and mopping might be the easier option. See you tomorrow."

Debbie's car pulled away, and Janet paused.

The night was still. As she gazed up, a brilliant meteor shot across the sky. Another one followed, then another.

The Leonids.

Debbie had mentioned them a few days ago. The sight of a night sky filled with stars, celestial dust swirling between galaxies, and the other forms of matter that made up God's great universe touched her heart.

No matter what strange things humans managed to cook up on Earth, God's gentle strength shone through everything around her. Sometimes she simply had to remind herself to pause and look up.

# CHAPTER FOURTEEN

*G*re you here to see Miss Eidenbach again?" Ashley peered at Janet over her glasses. The cheetah print frame set off the receptionist's vibrant personality.

"I am. I'm bearing gifts again, but on my own this time."

"Sometimes less is more." Ashley made a face, but it wasn't to make fun of the elderly woman. It was more like regretful compassion. "If we've got choices about growing older, I hope I keep smiling. But then I suppose not everyone's had a life to smile about, have they?" She tipped her head toward the solarium. "She's right over there again. I'm hoping today goes better for you."

But Janet had no sooner walked into the warm, welcoming room than Ann Marie stood up, grabbed her walker, and stomped out the opposite door.

Janet sighed.

She couldn't bring herself to chase the woman, but Ann Marie's reaction had to mean something. Was she upset that they had something from the house she'd lived in for decades? Or was it the letters themselves?

Janet glanced down at her watch.

She had ninety minutes free, and she was less than ten minutes from Charlie Briscoe's house.

Decision made.

She got into her car, set the cookies she'd intended for Ann Marie on the passenger seat, and drove to Charlie's place. She pulled up the drive and parked under a patch of old, majestic evergreens.

The house and barns were in good shape, but Mitchell Briscoe hadn't spared an extra dime to trick things out. The paint was matte, and the trim around the windows showed signs of peeling. It wasn't bad, but it wasn't all that great either. Maybe Charlie meant to keep it long enough to turn a land deal into money in the bank.

No one answered her knock. She tried the doorbell, but nothing happened when she pressed the button. She blew out a disappointed breath. She'd been ready to chat with him and get a feel for his character after all these years, but luck wasn't on her side today.

She began retracing her steps to the car—then drew up short when Charlie approached from the farthest barn.

He was strong, handsome, and in great shape for someone who'd spent twenty years in an office making himself and other people rich. He paused when he saw her, and then a welcoming smile transformed his face. "Janet?"

"Hey, Charlie."

He trotted to meet her and gave her a hug. "It's been so long. How are you? How's Ian? I've been back over a year, but I've been tied up making a mess of things here," he said with a grin. "What brings you over?"

"Cookies." She kept her tone bright. "I didn't want to bother you while you were settling in, but I thought it was past time to welcome you to the neighborhood."

"Except you don't live anywhere near this neighborhood," he pointed out, but he didn't refuse the cookies.

"Well, your name's been coming up the past few weeks, so I figured it was a nudge from the Holy Spirit to see how you like being back in the old hometown. And I should come right out and ask you why one of the Addisons' neighbors keeps seeing your truck parked up the road from the Addison farm."

He seemed unbothered by her directness. "Let's talk inside. Coffee?"

She shook her head. "I've had my limit for the day. But thank you."

He led the way up the stairs and opened the door for her.

Inside, the warm air seeped into her bones. She rubbed her arms. "I didn't realize how cold it had gotten."

He agreed, grabbed a coffee mug, and plugged a pod into the one-cup brewer. When his coffee was done, he settled into a kitchen chair.

Janet took the one opposite him, gazing around her. "You bought a farm, Charlie."

His expression was wry. "I sure did. Uncle Mitchell needed to sell, and I was ready to get out of the city. Try my hand at something else."

"And farming was the only option?" she asked. "There were no bagel shops available? Or cafés? That's what city guys usually do in the feel-good movies."

He laughed. "My mom loves those. She watches them all the time. There might have been coffee shops available, but I didn't look. I wanted to be back home and get my hands dirty again. Plus my mom's not well."

She hadn't expected that. "I'm so sorry to hear that."

"Us too. She was diagnosed with ALS and will need a lot of support. It's too much for Dad alone, Cassidy's got three kids in all kinds of high school sports, and I was ready to shift gears. I'd made my money on the Loop."

"The Loop?" she repeated.

"Chicago's business district," he explained. "It was time to switch things up. So I did. I helped Uncle Mitchell when I was a kid, so I thought I'd catch on quick, but farming isn't for the faint of heart. Uncle Mitchell had also let a lot of stuff go, though it wasn't by choice. It seemed like everything I touched broke down, so I reached out to Dani Addison for help. That's why my car's been over at the farm. Or my pickup truck, depending on what I'm driving at the time."

On a list of unexpected answers, Charlie's made the top. "You went to ask Dani's advice? She's coaching you?"

"She is. But quietly," he added. "We didn't want to get her father worked up. He didn't have anything nice to say about Uncle Mitchell and vice versa. He'd made a few comments to a friend about wishing the farm had gone out of Briscoe hands altogether, and I didn't want trouble. I just wanted some straight advice."

"I don't think there's anything on Claymont Creek Farm that Dani can't handle. She's amazing."

"You're not wrong." He took a long sip of his coffee then set the mug down. "I've got two new pieces of equipment ordered, and I contacted the agriculture department to get advice from them too. I've figured out that missing crucial dates by even a week means things don't grow, or they grow but don't produce. Either way, you've lost a year, and farms can't afford that. So Dani's been coaching me about what went wrong and how to fix things to make next year better. I made great money while I was away, but a failing farm can drain that funding faster than I would have believed. My goal is to keep my investments stable and make sure that doesn't happen. And Dani's been saving my bacon."

"Timing is everything." Janet stood. "I've got to get home, but it's been good to see you, Charlie. Thank you for being honest with me."

"My pleasure." He grinned again. When he did, Janet saw a flash of the high school football player she'd known. He tapped the package Janet had set on the table. "It snagged me some good cookies. I haven't gotten down to the depot yet, but Dani said you were a huge help to her when her ovens stopped working earlier this month."

"We were happy to do it. My mother jumped in too. It was an all-ovens-on-deck kind of situation."

Charlie followed her outside and down the porch steps.

"I'll be praying for your mom, Charlie. And all of you. Please reach out if there's anything we can do to help. I mean it. No one should feel alone during such a hard time."

"Not much anyone can do, but I appreciate the offer. Glad you stopped by, Janet."

"Me too." She got into the driver's seat, thinking.

Charlie had seemed like an unlikely person to do underhanded things like the vandalism at Claymont Creek Farm, but if it wasn't him or Hailey Adams or Rick Radner or even Dean Addison, who was it? Or was she being blinded by one of them and scratched them off the list too soon? She'd personally witnessed Charlie's conversation with Rick Radner, and it hadn't been an easygoing exchange of pleasantries. What had the two men been upset about? Dueling properties? Was that part of Charlie's plan to keep his investments stable?

She wasn't sure, but maybe Debbie's quiet discernment could show her something she couldn't see for herself. At this moment, she had no idea who might be involved in the farm's troubles, and that wasn't going to help Dani or her family at all.

Janet plunked a cup of coffee down beside Debbie on Saturday morning. "My endeavors got us nowhere. We have the same limited information we had two weeks ago about sabotage at the farm, except that no one seems to have done it. Unless we're being hoodwinked, and I'm beginning to think that's possible. Have I mentioned I'm very glad that Thanksgiving is late this year because it gives me more time to bake and stew about what I don't know?"

"Who could fool us to that extent?" Debbie sipped her coffee as she flipped bacon on the left side of the big griddle. "Not Dean. He's still conflicted, but I can't believe he's doing anything to hurt the family business. Even if he has his concerns."

"It could still be Hailey, I suppose. And Rick and Charlie were arguing over something. Could that something have been Claymont Creek Farm? That would mean one of them isn't being truthful, but I have no idea which one it is."

Debbie shrugged. "It could be any of the three. Hailey professes to admire the chickens' housing arrangements, but she could have let them loose to stir up trouble. Praising their amazing coop could be to throw us off. We know she's got a temper. But then who ran her off the road?"

"A big dark SUV. We have no way to know whether it was intentional."

"Exactly." Debbie nudged a batch of home fries off to the side then poured more onto the grill and spread them into a single layer. "And there's a gazillion of those around."

A sudden thought occurred to Janet. "If it really happened."

"We saw the results firsthand." Debbie frowned until she caught Janet's eye and realization dawned. "You mean what if she simply missed the curve and went off the road?"

"And concocted the story about the mysterious SUV to take suspicion off her," Janet said. "Let's say she releases the hens because she doesn't like the donkeys pulling carts."

"Which is such a shame, because it's a big draw during the fall and helps the farm's bottom line." Debbie added liberal amounts of chopped onion, parsley, paprika, salt, pepper, and garlic to the potato mixture. The mouthwatering aroma filled the air.

"Maybe we need to entertain the idea of multiple perps." Janet ducked out the swinging door to top off her coffee then returned in time for the timer to go off. She set down her mug and rushed to pull out perfectly browned muffins, adding to the heavenly smells in the kitchen. "One person who took the log splitter, because that's out-right theft and could be unrelated. Then someone like Hailey who's done all the other things to make this season difficult. It could be coincidental timing." Her phone dinged with a text that made her brighten up. "Ian's on his way in for coffee, and possibly some muf-fins or other goodies for the station."

"Keeping our officers happy is important." Debbie flipped the potatoes to ensure they wouldn't burn. "You could be right about at least two saboteurs. Which means Hailey's act is just an act and she's willing to risk jail to mess with the Addisons' farm. We know she's been heckling farmers up north. Have they dealt with vandalism too?"

That was a valid point. "We should take a ride up there and see what's what. Maybe Monday, since I've already talked to Charlie?"

"I'm tied up Monday," Debbie said. "Paulette and I are assembling Thanksgiving baskets for church. And your baking schedule is crazy with the holidays upon us."

It was. She'd taken orders for multiple holiday luncheons, celebrations, meetings, and even some corporate gift baskets of her pies, muffins, and pumpkin rolls. "You're right. I don't see a window of time between now and Thanksgiving to get up there. I was just thinking that if Hailey is responsible for the shenanigans at Claymont Creek Farm, wouldn't she be doing similar things to the farms she's targeted up there?"

"I've been thinking that myself." Ian came through the kitchen door, holding a travel mug that he'd likely filled from the pot behind the counter. "I'll take a ride up and nose around unofficially on Monday. I'm off then, and that might answer some questions."

"That would be wonderful," Janet told him. "We stay on schedule here, but we can still compare what's happening there with what's been going on here. Hailey lives between Sugarcreek and Dennison. If it's her pestering the Addisons, it makes sense she'd pester the others."

"Except their farms aren't open to the public like Claymont Creek Farm is," Ian reminded them. "She's demonstrated in front of several Amish and Mennonite places because they use horses for plowing and pulling buggies. She might not have easy access to mess things up for them."

"Normally, I'd agree with you, but I think she'd find a way. Thank you for checking it out either way. That's a huge help from our perspective. And here are some fresh muffins." Janet handed him a box she'd filled and kissed his cheek.

Ian grinned as he peeked inside. "Blueberry and chocolate chip. You've made the crew very happy this morning. I'll see you later."

Shortly after he left, Greg appeared at the kitchen door. Debbie's face lit up.

So did Greg's. "We still on for the Veterans Memorial Gala tonight?"

"We sure are." Debbie set a large roaster top over the potatoes and moved his way. "I can't wait. Honoring veterans is so important. Are the boys coming?"

"Yep. They're doing their homework this morning, and then they have basketball practice this afternoon, and tonight we'll all be able to go to the gala together."

"Wonderful."

"They made me promise not to keep them there for the dancing part," Greg added with a grin.

Debbie laughed. "Understandable."

Kim and several members of the museum board were hosting an event to honor not just the veterans who had come through Dennison in World War II but local veterans throughout the ages. There was a potluck supper, a presentation on the military and Dennison, and then dancing in the refurbished town hall. Kim had given Jim Watson access to her library of World War II-era music, from which he had made a playlist.

"But that's okay, as long as we're there," Greg continued. "The boys might not appreciate Glenn Miller. But their father does."

Debbie's cheeks flushed a becoming shade of pink. "Me too."

Janet reached for Greg's coffee mug, looking for an excuse to give them some privacy. "Can I fill that up for you?"

"Thank you," Greg replied.

She took plenty of time filling the coffee and doctoring it the way he liked. When she returned to the kitchen, Greg had his hand against Debbie's left cheek. "See you tonight."

"I can't wait."

After he left, Janet pretended to fan her face with one hand. "Whew! That man is smitten, my friend."

Debbie smiled dreamily. "Well, that makes two of us."

"I know." Janet met Debbie's smile with one of her own. "And I couldn't be happier for both of you, but Harry's here for breakfast, and I expect Crosby's got an appetite too. I'm hoping for a busy Saturday followed by a lovely evening celebrating our military and history."

It was a busy Saturday. Janet had just enough time to get home, shower, and unplug the six-quart slow cooker filled with homemade chicken stew. Ian had pulled into the driveway to pick her up when her phone rang. Lettie Karras's number appeared in the display.

Janet answered quickly. "Hey, Lettie. What's up?"

"An idea came to me while I was thinking about our conversation."

"What's that?"

"Ann Marie." She said the name slowly.

Ian stepped through the door, and Janet waved a greeting. "Your neighbor in Red Meyers's place."

"Yes. I thought it was strange. From the get-go." She sounded odd. As if getting the words out was difficult.

Alarm bells clanged in Janet's head. "Lettie?"

There was no answer.

"Lettie, are you there?" Janet called. She waved Ian back toward the car.

"Aren't we forgetting the stew?" he asked as they climbed inside.

"I'll have Mom get it. We're not going to the gala. We're heading to Lettie Karras's place." She held up her phone for him to see as it connected to his hands-free system. "She stopped talking, Ian. I think something happened to her."

Ian radioed for an ambulance, but they beat the ambulance there.

Lettie didn't answer the door, and she didn't poke her head out the window as she'd done before.

Nothing but silence greeted them.

They went around to the side door, and once again there was no answer. "Stand back, Janet." Ian broke the glass, reached in, and flipped the deadbolt to open the door. "Go to the front door. I'll open it and ditch my shoes on the steps. That way we're not tracking splintered glass through the house."

Janet met him at the front door a few seconds later. She dashed into the house, through the small living room and into the kitchen while Ian hurried to the second floor.

The kitchen was empty.

Then she remembered Lettie talking about her cozy first-floor bedroom. She hurried back across the living room and opened the bedroom door.

Lettie Karras lay on the old-fashioned double bed. Her phone was off to one side, still connected to Janet, but the elderly woman wasn't moving.

# CHAPTER FIFTEEN

anet gasped and hurried to the woman's side. "Ian, she's in the bedroom! Lettie, can you hear me?"

Lettie didn't stir.

An ambulance siren became audible, but as Janet leaned over Lettie's inert body, fear gripped her heart. Were they too late? Had Janet been the last person to speak to the gracious elderly woman?

She touched Lettie's hand. It was warm, and she breathed a sigh of relief.

Ian joined her and laid two fingers along Lettie's throat. "She's alive."

Janet's heart swelled with hope. "Ian, her words were a bit slurred when I spoke to her earlier. I think she had a stroke."

The paramedics streamed into the room.

Ian and Janet moved out of the way. "I was talking to her on the phone," Janet said to the paramedics. "Her voice got weird, and then she stopped talking. She might have had a stroke."

The EMTs wasted no time loading Lettie on a gurney. As they trundled her out of the house, the driver moved to Ian's side. "We're going straight to Union Hospital. They've got a full stroke protocol there. We don't want to take any chances."

"We'll let her family know," Ian replied.

Within seconds, the ambulance was gone.

Janet trembled while Ian got in touch with Lettie's granddaughter and told her what had happened. Then he pulled Janet into his arms.

"I'm being silly. There's no reason to be shaky now when I was fine while it was happening. What's the matter with me?" Tears streamed down her cheeks, and Ian grabbed a tissue from a box on the nightstand and handed it to her.

"You're amazingly normal," he reassured her. "Just like when Tiffany was little and needed stitches. You didn't fall apart until the whole thing was over. You had a brave face for her, and then you cried when everything was all right and she couldn't see you. Courage under pressure, and then a good release valve when the adrenaline wears off."

She gave a watery chuckle. "What did Lettie's granddaughter say?"

"She and her husband are going straight to the hospital. I told them I'd wait here for the window repair service to arrive. They'll board it up and then replace the glass on Monday. In the meantime, I'm going to clean up the glass on the floor."

"I'll hold the dustpan for you."

"Nothing like some teamwork to steady the nerves." He found the broom and the dustpan in a narrow kitchen closet. He handed her the dustpan and then went out to the car for the heavy gloves he kept in there. When he came back, he asked her, "Do you know Lettie?"

"She used to come into the bakery, years ago," Janet told him. "This was her house for a long time. She sold it some years ago and had a little apartment someplace until her granddaughter bought the house and invited Lettie to come live with her. For her, this house has always been home."

Ian carefully removed three larger pieces of glass. "But why would she call you after all this time?"

"We'd called on her to ask about the rental Red Meyers owned across the street. Lettie lived here around when we think those letters were written." Janet bent over to sweep shards of glass into the dustpan. "We wondered if she'd be able to tell us who they belonged to, but she couldn't. In fact, she told us that there were no married women living there except for the couple that lived in one half of the house, and the husband never served. The other side was rented to the Eidenbach family for over fifty years. She said that was a testimony to how good a landlord Red was, that people would stay in his places for generations. But then she mentioned that the Eidenbachs' daughter worked at the post office during that time. But also that she was single and never married."

"That sounds like a dead end."

Janet handed the broom to Ian. "Maybe not. Maybe Ann Marie Eidenbach rented a room or had another family living with her at some point. Anything's possible over a long stretch of time like that. But we do know that the letters went through the Dennison post office and ended up in a closet. Ann Marie Eidenbach was in both places, but why would she hide the letters? Why the subterfuge?"

"Perhaps the spouses' families hated each other." Ian carefully moved the broom across the floor. "That tale is as old as time."

"Maybe. But a nearby neighbor would probably have an inkling of that, wouldn't they?"

Ian arched a brow as he finished sweeping. "Do the Penallens know anything personal about us?"

He made a good point. The Penallens lived four doors down on the opposite side of the street from Janet and Ian. They'd been there for over fifteen years, and all they had was a friendly wave relationship. "Point taken. So even if Lettie wasn't what you'd call a private person, the Eidenbachs might have been."

"Not everyone wants to be gossip fodder, whether it's over the back fence or across social media."

They finished cleaning up the glass, and Janet called her mother and asked her to pick up the chicken stew. The emergency repair service truck pulled into the driveway and made quick work of the window. When they had the house locked up, Ian and Janet hurried to the car. The heavens opened, and a cold, hard, piercing rain splattered them as they raced across the street and clambered inside.

Ian started the engine then turned to Janet. "Gala? Or home?"

She didn't hesitate. "Home, please. I'm not up for a party after all of this. Even a really nice one. I'm too worried about Lettie. I don't want to think about what would have happened if she'd tried to call after I'd silenced my phone for the gala."

"Agreed." He patted her knee. "I think a great old movie and some comfort food are in order."

"Any one of our usual favorites will do," she said. "I want mindless entertainment."

"And I'll make popcorn the old-fashioned way."

"Perfect."

It wasn't the evening they'd planned, but hopefully they'd saved a life tonight. That made it an amazing night after all.

Ian walked into the café shortly before closing time on Monday.

The weather had grown cold. Light snow was forecast for the overnight hours. It wasn't expected to stick, but the march to winter was in full swing.

He leaned against the counter, dissatisfaction deepening the lines between his brows. "I struck out, and I honestly don't know if that's good or bad. I couldn't find a trace of anyone having similar problems at the farms near where Hailey lives. Eli Borgentrager and his whole family have helped build up that area. Eli always has his finger on the pulse of the farming community, and he's heard nothing about vandalism. They're all familiar with Hailey's rhetoric and her picketing, but nothing more than that."

"It doesn't make sense for her to be behind the incidents at Claymont Creek Farm then, does it?" Debbie emerged from cleaning the kitchen to help Janet finish the tables and the counter. "Why would her MO change?"

"That's just it," Ian replied. "That would be unusual. It doesn't completely rule her out, but it makes her less of a suspect."

"Which brings us back to our two upstanding businessmen or an unknown entity." Janet frowned. "I was kind of hoping you'd find something to narrow down the possibilities."

Before anyone could say anything else, the café door swung open and a blond woman came inside. "Janet Shaw?"

Janet took a step forward. "That's me. This is my husband, Ian, and my business partner and friend, Debbie Albright."

The woman smiled. "I'm Emily Brinkman, Lettie Karras's granddaughter. I wanted to come and thank you—thank you both," she added, gesturing to Ian. "You saved my grandmother's life the other night. If you hadn't gotten to her, I don't know what would have happened. We are so grateful."

"How is she doing?" Janet had been praying for a good outcome.

"So much better than she could have been," Lettie's granddaughter told her. "They had the right staff and the right medications at Union to help mitigate the stroke. They repeatedly told us that the timing was crucial. The fact that she was there within forty-five minutes of it happening made all the difference, and that was all due to you. So thank you from all three of us—me, my husband, and Granny. You saved her life."

"I'm glad she picked that moment to call me," Janet replied. "She was trying to tell me something, and her voice and tone kept getting worse and worse as she spoke. Then there was nothing."

"Sorry about the window," Ian added. "My choices were limited."

Emily waved that away. "They fixed it today. We're just glad you were able to respond so quickly. A window is a small price to pay for my grandmother being okay. Oh, and there's this." She withdrew a sheet of paper from the pocket of her jacket. "Granny had me write it down. She's struggling with thoughts and words, but it's clearing up, again thanks to you guys."

Janet took the folded sheet of paper. She unfolded it and read aloud, "'MIA husband. Story. Red's family. No husband.'" She frowned. "Did she happen to say anything else?"

Emily shook her head. "No. It makes no sense to me, but she was insistent that I pass that on. I assumed it would mean something to you."

"We'll figure it out. If it was important to Lettie, it's important to us," Janet assured her. "Keep us posted, all right?"

"I sure will. Thanks again." Emily left the café.

"My guess is that Red's family knows something after all," Janet told the others. "I don't know if Ann Marie had a husband that went MIA in Vietnam, but it's worth dropping by Callie Jo Meyers's fabric shop to talk with Abby. Callie Jo is Abby's daughter," she explained to Debbie. "She's a few years younger than us, so you probably don't remember her. Abby's a snowbird now. She stays with Callie Jo while she's up north over the summer, but she leaves for Florida soon, so we can't waste time."

"I'll lock the door and get my jacket." Debbie hurried away as Ian gave Janet a kiss goodbye.

"I would have loved being at the gala with the prettiest lass in the room," he said. "But saving a life was even better. Well done, Mrs. Shaw."

"I completely agree."

Janet and Debbie strolled into Callie Jo Meyers's quilt shop fifteen minutes later.

Callie Jo waved to them as they came in. She was figuring yardage with customers at the cutting table. "Hey, ladies. I'll be right with you. Feel free to browse while you wait." She quickly finished and came to join them. "What can I help you with?"

Janet took the lead. "Is your mom here?"

"Sure is. Piecing quilt tops like always right back there." Callie Jo pointed to the back of the store.

The fabric shop was a well-known entity in town, especially since Callie Jo had purchased a long-arm quilting machine, which quilters were happy to pay her to use on their pieced quilts. When it was quiet or she had someone else to cut cloth and run the register, she and her mother quilted in the back room.

"Please go on back," Callie Jo said. "I'll join you if I get a minute."

Janet and Debbie made their way to the back room, which was as cozy as most living rooms, with comfy furniture and a playlist of favorites going softly in the background.

Abby Meyers smiled a welcome. She wasn't the kind of person who had to be led into a conversation. She liked people and enjoyed talking to them. She motioned to a couple of chairs and started right in. "Now this is an unexpected pleasure." She kept sewing as she spoke, working a section by hand. Her experienced hands dropped quick, precise stitches in and out of a dusky rose calico. "Two best friends that time brought back together," she said warmly. "At my age, that makes my heart feel good. What brings you gals by?"

"That box of World War II artifacts you brought to the museum," Janet said.

"Of course." Abby's eyes crinkled at the corners as she remembered. "It was such a fun find. I've always said if you want something permanently lost, put it on the top shelf, way back, because most people won't go beyond what they can see from the floor. I'm pretty sure that held true for that box. What a treasure trove of notes, medals, recipes, and newspaper articles. It was in great shape too, completely untouched by mice or anything else. Now there's a testimony to my uncle, right? An old house, several tenants, and no mice. What were you wondering about?"

"The letters," Debbie said.

"In the packet?" Abby frowned. "I didn't get into them. They seemed private, you know? I'm not one to snoop, and Ann Marie Eidenbach has always been a very private person."

"We reached out to Lettie Karras about the letters and the people who lived in that house. She shared some interesting information, but then she tried to get a message to me on Saturday night."

"And you and Ian hurried right over there and saved her." When Janet blushed, Abby paused long enough to pat her arm then went right back to stitching. "No sense getting embarrassed. I'm just glad you were on the phone with her at the right moment. Providential timing, that's what I call it."

Janet nodded agreement. "It was. Her granddaughter stopped by a little while ago with a note from Lettie, possibly with what she was trying to tell me. But it held scattered words rather than a comprehensive message. We were hoping to run it by you before the holiday. I know you generally spend Thanksgiving with your son's family in North Carolina before heading down to Florida for the winter."

"I'm actually doing the first leg tomorrow," Abby replied. "That way I'm there to spend a few days with my grandkids. I'm glad to help you if I can. Do you have the note?"

Janet withdrew the sheet of notepaper from her pocket. "It's kind of cryptic."

Abby poked the needle into a nearby pincushion and then read the note. "I remember snatches of this story, but it's from a long time ago. My mother and a couple of neighbors were talking about Ann Marie."

Janet scooted forward on her chair, eager to hear the tale.

"We hated to make Ann Marie move out of Uncle Red's place," Abby went on. "She wasn't one bit happy about it, but we felt like we had no choice. She needed more care than she was getting, living on her own in a two-story rental. She couldn't do stairs anymore, and the place was too much for her."

"She's getting excellent care at Good Shepherd," Debbie assured her. "What story did you overhear from your mother about her?"

"I was just a girl. My mother and two other women—Lettie and another woman named Collette Franz—had come to our house, and they were talking about how they were sorry for Adalyn Eidenbach because it couldn't be easy to have a grown daughter there, making up stories. I was reading in the corner, and they must have forgotten I was in the room."

"What kind of stories?" Janet pressed.

Abby sat back and pursed her lips. "The daughter was pretending her husband was MIA. She even got one of those MIA flags you put up outside, and everybody thought she was doing it to show her support for families of missing soldiers. But then she told people that her husband was missing in action."

Janet and Debbie exchanged startled glances.

"Except there was no husband. She was single. Never even had a beau according to the ladies, and then, as my mother was saying that Ann Marie maybe wasn't quite right in the head, someone made a noise at the open window." She drew a deep breath and sighed. "It was Ann Marie's mother." She bit her lip. "That's why I remember it so vividly. The look on her face was so awful. I felt dreadful for her, hearing her daughter gossiped about that way. If Ann Marie truly was sick, why wouldn't folks choose to be kind, both toward her and her family?"

"That's an age-old question," Debbie told her. "She had no husband but pretended she did?"

"So I gathered, but that's about all I know." Abby's reading glasses had slid down her nose. She took them off and set them aside before continuing. "They shouldn't have been talking about her. Gossip can be such a terrible thing, and they knew it. Even I knew it, although I was so young. But the expression on Mrs. Eidenbach's face—she was heartbroken to catch people she liked and should have been able to trust talking about her daughter that way."

"I don't blame her," Janet murmured.

"I've never forgotten that look. I don't know if they ever patched up their friendship. I can't imagine they did, and Ann Marie lived there alone all those years after her parents died. She kept to herself, and after what my mother did, I can't blame her. She must have felt as if she lived in a den of vipers."

"Did she take the MIA flag down?" Janet asked.

"The pole was taken down a few years later. My dad had to help Uncle Red dig it up. It had been set in concrete to stabilize it, but over the years the pole had rusted badly and needed to be removed," Abby said. "I never heard any more talk about anyone missing in action, but I'm sure that conversation is what Lettie was referring to. It was the kind of awkward moment that sticks with you."

"And yet, the letters were written to 'My dearest wife,'" Janet told her. "So maybe there was a husband after all?"

Abby hesitated, as if trying to figure out how to word her answer. "A person can make up all kinds of things to support this belief or that when life doesn't turn out the way you want it to. Letters can be written and sent from wherever. For all I know, Ann Marie could have written those letters herself. What I do know is that there was no husband that anyone knew of. After a while, everyone stopped talking about it. I think if he existed but went missing in action, he wouldn't have been shrugged off that way. Ann Marie would have fought to keep his memory alive." She shook herself as if loosening such unpleasant thoughts. "Would you ladies like a cup of coffee? Or hot cocoa?" She indicated a coffee station on a nearby table against the wall. "That nip in the air necessitates hot chocolate to me."

"I'd love to, but I need to get home." Janet stood.

Debbie stood also. "And I'm riding with her, but I want to thank you, Abby. You've been a big help. Have a safe trip and a lovely Thanksgiving."

"You're welcome, both of you. Same to you."

They said goodbye to Callie Jo on the way out.

When they were back in the car, Debbie raised her eyebrows. "Curiouser and curiouser."

Janet started the engine. "I couldn't have said it better myself. How is it that the more we learn, the less we seem to know?"

# CHAPTER SIXTEEN

eans, motive, and opportunity." Janet checked off her fingers as she spoke. "Ann Marie was allegedly pretending to have a husband. She was inventing personal drama in her life. Her motive for taking the letters, if that's what she did, is unclear. How would she know they were love letters unless she opened and read them? And what would have prompted her to do that? So maybe she did write them to herself."

"I didn't want to say it in there," Debbie said, "but there's no way she could do that and get a military postmark, right? It was definitely war mail or overseas airmail. And we both know that everybody dies famous in a small town. I expect that was true then too. You either knew everyone or you knew of them. Ann Marie had the opportunity to steal them because she sorted the letters. She'd know who they were from and who they were going to, so she would probably have guessed at the content."

"This whole theory means some woman never got the beautiful love letters her husband wrote to her." Janet frowned. "They might have been his last words to her. We don't know who it is, and we don't know if the soldier came home."

"But Ann Marie knows." Debbie met Janet's gaze. "I don't want to push an old lady, but she would be the only person who knows where those letters should have gone. No one except the soldier knew they existed, and we don't know if he lived or died. She's our one link."

Janet had to agree, but the thought of chasing down a fragile old woman had no appeal. "Judging by Ann Marie's reaction to us, and then later to me, I think we need to leave her alone. We can't pester a woman at her age when she clearly doesn't want to see us. We might have to let this puzzle go."

"I hate to agree, but I think you're right." Debbie put the car in gear. "We should table this one because there are some pots that maybe shouldn't be stirred."

She dropped Janet off at the depot.

Janet's car didn't even have time to warm up on the short drive from the depot to her driveway. She parked and hurried into the house.

Laddie had been sleeping. Maybe dreaming. When Janet latched the door behind her, the little dog bounced up and barked frantically, as if chagrined to be caught sleeping on the job.

"Laddie, leave it," Ian commanded.

The dog stared up at him then looked at Janet. Recognition calmed his frenzied awakening. He dashed up to her and danced around her legs.

"You're a good boy." She gave him a thorough petting because she'd been gone all day. Their cat, Ranger, didn't care when she came or went, but Laddie did. She straightened and said, "Supper smells amazing."

"Chicken and rice. Comfort food. I take it you didn't have much luck with Abby Meyers?"

"We did okay." She peeled off her jacket, hung it on the coatrack, and perched on a kitchen stool. "But we've realized we can't go further with Ann Marie because she's kind of fragile. It doesn't seem fair to dredge up sixty years of bad memories at this stage of her life."

"On the other hand, a guilty conscience isn't something most of us want to take to the grave," Ian reminded her.

Janet frowned. "I agree, but it's a fine line between investigating and pressing too hard. I have to let it go for now. We tried." She accepted the glass of sparkling water he handed her with a murmured thanks. "We didn't fail. We called the game on account of a possible emotional storm."

"We had many an October soccer game go that route, except it was for a possible thunderstorm." Ian clinked his glass with hers. "There are times when you have to take a step back. That can be one of the hardest aspects of an investigator's job. Can you grab a couple of plates?"

She crossed to the cupboard and was lifting the plates when her phone rang. Jim Watson's number flashed in the display. She answered at once. "Hey, Jim. What's up?"

"I've got a yes from both of Kim's brothers, and three of their children!" he exulted.

"Neal and Marcus?"

"And their wives. Eileen's grandkids that still live here were easy, but we've also got four grandkids coming in from the Dallas area. Plus one granddaughter's new baby. Kathy had to refuse because her husband is too ill to travel, and she doesn't want to leave him."

Kathy was Kim's older sister.

"But her daughter, Alicia, is coming, which means there will be a table full of people there on Thursday."

"I'm providing dessert," Janet told him. "Are they surprising Kim? Or letting her know they're coming?"

"Neal and Marcus decided to tell her that they're coming so she doesn't fret that no one will be there, but they're keeping the extended family on the down low. I'll make sure the food order is right, though," he added. "Kim's having it catered so she can relax with family. I'll keep the caterer apprised of the real numbers."

"Jim, that's marvelous." Janet couldn't wait to let Debbie know the good news. "Kim will be thrilled."

"I know." Satisfaction rang through his tone. "Traveling during the holidays isn't for the faint of heart, but those Palmer boys are made of tough stuff. They'll be fine. I did have to hear Marcus talk about his dislike of airports three separate times. But he loves his mother more than he dislikes the crowds, so they're in."

"Thank you, Jim."

He laughed. "No thanks needed. I've already decided I'm crashing their party to have Thanksgiving dinner with them. I don't know how much more time I'll get with them at our ages, so I'm grabbing what I can while they're in town. It will be good to catch up with them, and good for them to see how much has changed in the town. The lights, the new houses, how the museum has grown, the skating rink, and the flags on the light poles. I'm glad they're getting a chance to come back and see it."

"Me too." She didn't miss the pride in Jim's voice. He'd stood strong for Dennison and Uhrichsville for decades. He'd kept things upbeat when the trains shut down and when manufacturing sites closed as work was assigned overseas. Jim had devoted his life to unifying their little town. "Good job, my friend."

"Thank you. See you soon."

Ian had been listening from his seat at the table. "You went from morose to delighted in the space of a phone call."

Janet laughed. "Not morose. Resigned. There's a big difference. But yes, I'm thrilled that Jim was able to make headway with Kim's family. We get to check that off our list, other than making pies and cream puffs for the Palmer crew. And I'm happy to do that, knowing Eileen will be surprised and Kim will be delighted." She sank into a chair and smiled at him. "However, at this moment, I'm just going to enjoy this wonderful meal."

"That took all of twenty minutes to make." Ian indicated the boxed mix in the recycling tote.

Janet handed him her plate. "Doesn't matter. I didn't have to do it, and right now this looks like haute cuisine to me, even if it started in a box. I have pledged to myself to leave worry on the back burner for the next week."

Ian raised a skeptical eyebrow at her.

"Mostly, anyway," she amended. "I'm going to focus on baking, Thanksgiving, Tiffany and her friends being here for four days, and getting through a packed weekend. Tiffany promised to help with the Christkindl booth, and she and the girls aren't heading back to school until late Saturday. They'll be here to see us light up the town."

"Good," Ian said. "Tiffany will love that."

"She will," Janet agreed. Then a new thought sent her mood falling again. "Wait a minute. Dani will be in the thick of her holiday sales from this point on, and that preoccupation will leave them ripe for shenanigans. I think whoever has been messing with the farm will act sooner rather than later, because weather's a big factor around here in December."

"You might be right, but it sure would help if we had a motive, Janet. Who stands to gain by messing with the Addisons?"

He made a good point. Try as she might, Janet still couldn't come up with a clear-cut motive. "I don't know of anyone who's angry with them except for Hailey, and that's not directed at them specifically. She targets anyone who she feels is mistreating animals. If it's not Hailey, then the other indicators are about land. But unless Rick or Charlie is lying, I still don't have any suspects."

Ian lifted one shoulder. "Wouldn't be the first time someone shrouded things to get what they want. Things don't always go to the highest bidder. Sometimes they go to the person who plays his or her cards the best. But this week's going to be hectic. Maybe things will clear up once things calm down after the holiday weekend."

"I remember saying that to my grandma years ago," Janet replied. "That this or that would get better when things calm down. She told me, 'Honey, the fact is things never really calm down. We learn to roll with it because that's life.' At the time I thought she was wrong." Janet set out silverware and took her seat. "She wasn't, and it was a great lesson. But having said that, I'm glad Tiffany and the girls will be here for the Christkindl Market and the town lighting. I'm glad for the busyness of the whole thing. It will make a nice new tradition."

The weekend events were new. The town hoped to make it an annual gathering, and it was a wonderful way to put the holiday season in full swing. The event offered a couple of hours to cruise the town, visit with shop owners and friends, and then gather for the tree lighting and old-fashioned caroling. The beautiful Nativity would be a perfect focal point in the brightly lit gazebo in the town's center.

"Mom and Dad are setting up the tent they bought for both events," Janet went on. "Dad said keeping his girls safe from the elements is priority one because taking care of us makes him happy. Plus I think the more he puts the thing up and takes it down, the easier it gets."

"Your dad's one tough guy." Ian brought the food to the table and slid into his seat. "That tent doesn't own a single easy component, despite what it says on the box. It's a four-person operation. But one thing about your dad is that he never gives up. A quality he managed to pass on to my beautiful wife." He reached for her hand to say grace. "And that's just another reason to love her."

"That was an amazing number of baked goods going out the door." Janet emphasized the words by sweeping her hand across her forehead as Paulette flipped the Closed sign into place Wednesday afternoon. "Well done, ladies. Now we all get to go home and cook some more."

Debbie and Paulette both laughed, as did Charla Whipple, Janet's former boss from Third Street Bakery. Charla had come over to offer her help and expertise.

She dusted her hands over her apron then untied it. "I love that you call on me to help during busy times, but I don't miss doing this all week long. Still, while full-on retirement suits my husband, I love putting in time here, Janet. You and Debbie have done a marvelous job.

But there's truth in your statement. I need to get home and get some family favorites prepared for tomorrow. I'll come back in Friday night to do cookies for Saturday. Happy Thanksgiving, everyone." She gave Janet a quick hug before hurrying out with two pies in her hands.

The café itself hadn't been too busy that day, which had actually been a blessing. It had given Paulette the time to help package and label pies, loaves, cakes, and breads. Between the four of them, they'd managed to fill all their outstanding Thanksgiving orders.

"I'm glad we finished the muffin orders yesterday," Debbie said as she finished wiping down the kitchen. "That made last night and today so much easier."

"And you learned how to roll a mean pie crust." Paulette grinned as she stacked Kim's order near the door. "But I am glad neither one of us has to go home tonight and bake pies for tomorrow." She indicated their boxed pies with a tap of appreciation. "With these and your mother's pretzel-bottom gelatine salad, we're all set for a wonderful dessert table."

"Now if I can manage to not overcook or undercook the turkey." Debbie groaned and buried her face in her hands.

Paulette nudged her with a laugh. "Overcooked makes the gravy taste richer, and undercooked means we put it back in the oven for a little while. Worst-case scenario, we'll eat dessert first, and that's not exactly a crime, is it?" Her smile remained firmly in place, but gentle understanding laced the older woman's tone. "I've done both, and we've all lived to tell the tale."

Janet wasn't sure if Paulette understood the impact of her kind words, but she saw the effect on Debbie. The crease between her brows relaxed, and the tension seeped from her shoulders. She moved toward the door. "I've got our pies."

Paulette was close behind. "And I'm dropping Kim's off with Jim." She lifted three pies.

Janet hefted the other four—two more for Kim's big crew and two for her own table. "I'll take these to your car and head on home. The girls will be there in less than two hours." She grinned at the other women as Debbie locked the door behind them. "That's when my holiday begins."

Except when she pulled into her driveway five minutes later, Tiffany's car was already there.

Janet burst out of her car and hurried up the walk.

Tiffany threw the door open and met her with a big hug. Janet hugged her back, excited. Then she held her at arm's length. "You look wonderful, sweetie! But you're here early, and I don't have food ready for you. I was going to whip up a bunch of your favorites."

"Don't worry. Dad ordered food." Tiffany led the way inside to include her friends. "He asked what we wanted, and we said—"

"Anything but pizza!" Tiffany's two friends sang out in unison, and all three burst out laughing.

Tiffany offered a quick explanation. "A water main broke near the university two days ago. Without clean water, they couldn't cook like they normally do, so it's been a mad rush on pizza of every kind you can imagine. That meant the shops were mobbed with students and townies alike, when they had anticipated pretty much everyone leaving on Wednesday. They'd downscaled their topping orders, so they were all running out of everything. It was crazy."

"One shop went to every local grocery store they could and bought pepperoni and mozzarella," one friend chimed in.

"Gross, gummy mozzarella," Tiffany added.

"Fewer students on campus should mean fewer pizzas," Janet said. "It was a reasonable assumption on their part until one catastrophe threw everything up in the air."

"Exactly. Now you've got to meet the girls. Wait, you met Fiona last year."

"I sure did." Janet clasped Fiona's hands between hers. "Welcome back, Fiona. I'm so glad you're here."

"And this is Fiona's older and much wiser sister, Ava." Tiffany laughed.

Ava smiled. "Thanks so much for having us, Mrs. Shaw. We're grateful. Fee and I always loved the idea of coming up here for school, even though Mom warned us that getting back and forth to Florida wouldn't be a piece of cake. Of course, she was right."

"Don't you hate when that happens?" Janet chuckled. "You know how those moms are."

The sisters laughed, and Fiona said, "It will make it all that much sweeter when we go home for Christmas break. That's only three weeks away, and there are plenty of things to keep us busy between papers, semester projects, and finals. So this is wonderful, Mrs. Shaw. Thank you for making it possible. I know our mom is relieved."

"She had this horrific image of an empty school and her two desolate girls sitting alone in cold, drafty rooms, dreaming of homemade turkey while we suffered with ramen," Ava added. "We're going to call her tomorrow and pretend to cook with her. I'll miss bustling around the kitchen with her."

"You're welcome to do more than pretend here," Janet assured them. "Tiffany has offered to help her dad serve at the free dinner the church is hosting."

Fiona's face lit up. "Can we help with that too?"

Ava joined in her sister's request. "Honestly, that would be amazing. I've never done anything like that before, but it sounds like the perfect way to start a Thanksgiving celebration."

"The more the merrier." Tiffany turned back to Janet. "We're not getting the food for two hours, Mom. Is there anything we can help with now?"

"Can you guys grab the pies out of the back seat? And then I need sweet potatoes washed and roasted, and bread broken for stuffing."

"On it." The three girls headed for the car while Janet started a fresh pot of coffee.

She'd told her friends that her holiday would start when Tiffany got home.

It certainly had. And to have the three girls around for a busy weekend, well, who could ask for more than that?

# CHAPTER SEVENTEEN

Janet frowned as she and Debbie packed totes for the Christkindl Market on Friday morning.

Debbie's dad was overseeing transportation. Debbie's mom was working at the clinic, so Janet's mother had agreed to run the booth. Ava and Fiona had requested study time, but Tiffany had offered to help her grandmother at the open-air market. Paulette and Debbie would run the café, and Janet would keep right on baking to cover the café, today's booth, their booth for Light Up the Town, and the depot's first Christmas Train weekend. Kim had ordered two cookies for each train passenger, which made Charla's agreement to bake overnight with her an answer to prayer.

"This feels weird." Janet locked down the cover on the filled plastic tote.

"What's weird about it?" Debbie asked.

"It feels like we're branching out. Testing the waters. And both of our mothers are so excited about doing this that they're probably going to pester us to enter more festivals and events. I'm afraid of trying to take on too much too fast."

"My mom *is* pretty delighted about coming over to help when she's done at two." Debbie closed the lid on her tote and quirked a brow. "Since when is excitement a bad thing?"

"That depends." Janet lifted her tote to place it with the others. "I'm fine with doing it, and it's great when Charla can be here, but it would have been very tough to get through without her. There's only so much I can do, even with a great setup like ours. But I do like the exposure we're getting with these booths."

"I was thinking the same thing," Debbie said as she stacked half a dozen cookie sleeves into the next tote. "About a bakery helper, I mean. Maybe Charla would consider doing more hours for us. I can't pretend to be a good backup for you. I love that our mothers have been willing to help, but they're busy with other things. I first thought of it when we said yes to supplying Hummingbird Acres with cookies and cupcakes for their Christmas Bazaar, because it puts a lot of pressure on you if Charla isn't available. That's not fair."

Hummingbird Acres was an eclectic co-op set up in a gorgeous old barn south of town. Marcy Gayle had opened her home to her husband's eccentric aunt, Winifred Gayle. Winnie was an elderly woman whose memory was as interesting as her past. Marcy's daughter, Claire, was a year younger than Tiffany. She'd stayed home to get her degree at the community college and help her mother launch the cooperative. It had been a good choice for both of them.

"I like helping Marcy and Claire at the cooperative. And I love being able to chat with Winnie, even if it's a short visit. There's something about her that draws me in."

Debbie interrupted her with her typical wisdom. "She brings the past to life."

"You got that right."

"Marcy said Winnie is excited to be overseeing the cookie sale." Debbie adjusted her boxes to pack her tote tighter. "It makes me feel good to think of her being busy, not sitting around wishing her life were different."

Winnie, the youngest of three girls, had always been the odd duck, in her own words. Different, creative, and most particular. She used to tell her family that she didn't belong with them, that she wasn't one of them.

No one had listened, of course.

She was a child when she first said it, but she'd persisted in that belief all her life. That she was different. Then a DNA test nearly two years ago had proven that Winnie was right.

She wasn't a Gayle. She wasn't related to them at all, but how does one approach that kind of truth to a somewhat delicate older woman when she'd inherently sensed the difference all along?

Janet had no idea how Marcy and her husband had handled that. Had it brought peace to the elderly woman's mind? Or simply upset her when no change could be had?

She was sure it had been a tough reckoning, either way.

"I feel guilty every time you come in early or stay late." Debbie went on to fill her next tote with loaves of pumpkin and banana bread, two local favorites. "I haven't even asked when you slept last. Should we say no to extra business? We're not flush, but we're not hurting for money."

Janet snorted. "We never say no to business. We don't need to grow big, but it's good to get our name out there, especially leading into winter. Everything slows down from January through March. I'll have plenty of time to rest then. Name recognition keeps customers calling in orders and stopping by. I think we'll be fine with Charla's help. I honestly don't know how I would have gotten prepped for this weekend without her. I'm not what you'd call an anxious person—"

Debbie laughed. "True words. You are about as calm as they come."

Janet grinned. "Thank you. But I like being ahead of the curve, and an extra set of hands when we're bombarded with orders and customers will make that possible." She lifted her tote and carried it out to join the other ones they'd filled.

It was quieter than a typical Friday morning. The usual weekday coffee crowd wasn't out and about on the holiday weekend. The extra calm hours were a blessing today, and Janet was sending up a prayer of gratitude about that when Troy Henry came through the door.

Paulette attempted to guide Troy to a seat, but he had other ideas. He crossed to where the women were packing the last tote of holiday goodies—pumpkin whoopie pies stuffed with cream cheese frosting. Then he folded his arms. "I know you two have been poking your noses into things up around the Addison place."

Janet hid a wince. There were only two customers in the café right now, but she'd been around long enough to know that a conversation with Troy could take interesting turns that weren't always valued in the court of public opinion. Even two eavesdroppers could fuel the small town's grapevine.

She motioned toward the door. "Let's talk by the ticket window."

To her surprise, he didn't argue. He followed her and Debbie to the old-fashioned waiting room outside the museum's ticket office.

"What can we help you with, Troy?" Debbie asked.

He frowned. "Something weird is going on over by Claymont Creek Farm."

Janet stayed quiet. Sometimes it was better to let Troy take the lead. Today was no exception.

"I got wind of people looking at land. Nosing around. I knew if those start-up companies got the town's blessing in New Philadelphia that we'd see growth here. I like growth," he said. "I make money from customers, same as you, but also from investments. I'm not sure what's going on over there, but it's something, and I'm worried it'll affect that growth we all like so much."

"Something like… what?" Janet prompted.

Troy grimaced. "I'm not sure, but people won't talk to me when I know for a fact they've talked to someone else—someone with deep pockets, mind you."

An image of Charlie Briscoe sprang into Janet's mind.

"That makes me wonder what they've got planned," Troy said. "What is it they want to do once the purchase is complete? And what kind of presentation will they make to the zoning board to get a green light on their project? A lot of developers know how to pretty the pot, if you get my drift. They do something helpful on one project to get approval on another. That's not bad business as a rule, but it can go bad if the wrong hands are involved. I appreciate the big city for a visit, but I'm a small-town kind of guy at heart. I don't want to see some rich bigwigs moving in and suddenly ruling the roost because they can buy and sell more than anyone else here."

"You think Charlie's doing something underhanded?" Janet hated to think it, but if Troy was right—and unpleasant as he could be, he wasn't often wrong…

"Charlie Briscoe?" Troy's brows shot up. "He's got something bad going on? Like what?"

"I thought that's who *you* were referring to," Janet explained. "I thought you were hinting that Charlie was caught up in some scheme."

"Our Charlie?" Troy shook his head. "Never in a million years. I watched that boy guide a football team to a state crown back in the day. Charlie's as honest as the day is long. I worked with his daddy when we were both young and starting out. I was investing in property while Dave Briscoe invested in family. I might have more money in the bank, but I'm at an age where I realize that Dave might've had the better idea. He's been a dad, a husband, a teacher, and a grandpa, and everyone loves him. No, it wasn't Charlie I was talking about. It was EDFC."

Debbie inhaled sharply. "Erie Development Financing Corporation in Cleveland? That corporation enticed all kinds of people to go in on developments both on the waterfront and outside the stadiums, and then ducked out the back door when it all fell apart. They walked away without a scratch because of cleverly written contracts while a bunch of local people lost their shirts. It was a mess."

"But what would a big entity like that want with Claymont Creek Farm? And would they really mess with the Addisons? That doesn't make sense."

"That's just it," Troy told her. "They wouldn't. They're too big. But someone smaller might stir the pot to get the ball rolling. Anyone who knows about EDFC's past wouldn't trust them if they cared about their community. But if you've got someone who doesn't care— well, you know what that means."

"Actually, I don't," Janet admitted.

"People who don't care are willing to take the money and run," Troy said. "They let things fall as they may. I don't know who's involved, but I've seen dirty dealing like this in the past. Some folks get greedy enough to do whatever it takes to strike their deal, no matter who gets hurt." He checked his watch then snugged his hat into place. "I need to get to an appointment about some rentals, but I wanted to catch you gals before this gets out of hand. The Addisons are good people. But I think there's a skunk out their way, and it's stinking to high heaven."

"A skunk?" Janet faced Debbie as Troy headed out the door. "As in, someone trying to court EDFC?"

Before Debbie could reply, customers streamed through the outer doors, and the women had to table their discussion until later.

By the time they closed and got over to the Christkindl Market, it was teeming with people.

"It was even busier when we opened at noon," Janet's mom, Lorilee, told them as Becca Albright placed several containers of baked goods into an old-fashioned brown paper bag with corded handles for a happy customer. The bags reminded Janet of vintage Christmas movies and times gone by.

Seeing how many people in the crowd held those bags told her that the sale was hugely successful, even before she crunched the numbers. The rack of shelves Janet's dad had put inside the tent was almost empty, and the twin folding tables, so handy for outdoor events, had only a few dozen offerings remaining.

"The organizers have outdone themselves." Debbie gazed at the other booths. "How about if you moms take a break and go explore for a bit?"

Becca laughed and handed off her apron. "I've been here for barely an hour but I'm dying to check things out."

"Tiffany's friends texted her that they were done studying, so she went home to pick them up," Lorilee added. "She wanted to give them a chance to see what the Christmas market is all about." She followed Becca's lead and removed her apron. "Back in a few. We'll bring you back a treat."

"I'm never opposed to treats," Janet assured her. "Especially if they include funnel cakes."

"You've loved those since we took you to your first fair as a toddler," Lorilee said fondly.

The two women ducked out and disappeared into the happy crowd of shoppers. When they returned about thirty minutes later with the promised funnel cake, Janet and Debbie made a lap around the market while they split the treat.

They were into the final ninety minutes of the well-attended event. Many of the vendors were running low on items. A few had run out and were packing things up. One such vendor was Dani Addison.

"We totally sold out." She smiled at them as her oldest nephew gathered empty totes to take to their van. "It was a wonderfully successful event."

"That's what we like to hear," Janet said. "You especially deserve it after everything you've been through lately."

"Thanks, Janet. I'm praying for no more hiccups. I'm ready for some smooth sailing."

"I don't blame you." Janet motioned at Dani's tent. "Do you want help breaking down your setup?"

"I've got Brady here, so we're all set, but thank you. If you're looking for empty calories, the funnel cakes are amazing."

Janet laughed. "Great minds think alike. Our moms just brought us some. Talk to you soon."

By the time Debbie and Janet got to the end of the market, the crowd was beginning to thin. The day was calm. The temps had hovered in the low fifties, but now that the sun had gone down, the night was growing cold.

As they turned to head back to their tent, Janet saw Brady Addison pull up to the near corner. Dani's van came up the road and paused at the intersection too. She took a left, and as she did, a big dark SUV rolled out of a small parking lot up the road.

Janet was too far away to read the plate, but in a moment of inspiration she pulled out her phone and zoomed in. She had just enough time to snap a picture of the rear of the car as it also turned left after Dani's van.

"What's up?" Debbie asked.

"That vehicle was like the one that was in my driveway. I wanted to get a shot of the license plate just in case." Janet opened the photo. "Gotcha, CHMP 99."

"You think it's Charlie?"

Janet shrugged. "Not too many people brought home a state title in football in ninety-nine. But why was he here?"

Debbie gave her a skeptical look. "Because it's a town event and there were things to buy? Because he's trying to support local businesses? Because he likes funnel cakes, same as we do?"

"I hate that you're making sense right now when all I can see is some kind of nefarious possibility about a guy with a great reputation." She tucked her phone away as they continued back to their booth. "Troy insists Charlie's not involved. And there are understandable reasons for his car being seen at Claymont Creek Farm. He was open about that. Dani seemed shocked that I'd even suggest him as a suspect, so why do I keep having a nagging thought that there's something else going on there? What is it about his behavior that's setting off my inner alarms? Or am I simply frustrated because the Addisons are being targeted and it feels like we're getting nowhere in stopping it?"

"I'm leaning toward that last one." Debbie tucked her arm through Janet's as they reached their booth. "At this moment I don't want to think about anything but the two cute guys waiting for us, ready to help take things down and put them away. Then we all get to go out to dinner together, and that's what I call a perfect ending to a wonderful day."

Debbie was right.

And she was probably spot-on about Charlie too. Before this all happened, he'd have ranked low on Janet's list of underhanded people. But despite everyone's beliefs about him, Janet sensed something amiss. Charlie's car, or one like it, had been identified at a number of places affecting the Addisons the past few weeks—and longer, according to Dani's neighbor.

Were all those sightings coincidental?

Maybe.

But maybe they weren't, and that was something she couldn't get out of her mind. How many of them could truly be explained by Charlie getting help from Dani?

Ian had said something about too many pieces for the puzzle, but she started pondering the pieces related to the Addisons' displays.

Things close to the road like the donkey pen, the torched frame, and even the henhouse. If Troy was right, and someone was trying to stir things up, Janet was pretty sure the display areas would be the easiest targets. Was it a coincidence that they were also the most noticeable?

She brought up her concerns to Ian that night. The girls were at the movies, and Janet had another early start the next morning, but she couldn't wait. "How was your day, dear?"

"Fine." He arched an eyebrow. "You want something." He had a college football game on and a book open on his lap, but she was pretty sure neither one held his attention. His huge yawn confirmed her suspicions.

She didn't deny it as she sat beside him on the sofa. "Nothing major."

He stretched. "Let's have it, then."

"Can you adjust the trail cams at Claymont Creek Farm to point more at the road, so they capture the area between the barns and the street?"

He tipped his head. "The Addisons have farm equipment worth thousands behind the barn. That's a lot of potential damage with no eyes on it."

"I know they do."

"Then why risk it?" Ian asked.

"I think this person wants things to be noticed. The Addisons kept quiet about the wood splitter, the plumbing issue, and the bad gas."

"True."

"So maybe the initial vandalism fell short of the goal. Maybe what our saboteur wants is to create a *noticeable* stir. Maybe the goal isn't some kind of vendetta but a mission to create visible havoc."

Ian frowned but didn't dismiss her logic. "It *was* a pretty solid escalation."

"Maybe the initial attempts didn't attract the desired attention." She explained what Troy had told them that morning. "The vandal might be trying to spook the locals to make it easier for a big corporation to swoop in and buy."

"I'll adjust the cameras first thing in the morning," Ian said. "I won't go up the main road either. I'll park off the road and go in the back way. That way no one sees me. The chances of anyone coming by at that time are small, but I'd rather be safe than sorry. I won't even tell the Addisons I'm there."

"Total stealth maneuvers," she quipped.

He his eyes twinkled at her as he indicated the wall clock with a thrust of his chin. "You've got another early start in the morning. I'm going to hang out here and wait up for the girls. Not because they need it, but because I do."

She kissed him good night. "You're a good man, Ian Shaw."

Charla was handling the overnight cookie baking for tomorrow's events. Between the Christmas Train and the lighting festival, they'd need a lot of cookies tucked into their little wax paper sleeves. Having Charla come in for a night shift was the difference between being tired and frantic and being prepared. In Janet's book, prepared was always better.

# CHAPTER EIGHTEEN

Kim's smile was the first thing Janet noticed when the museum director came through the café door the next morning. She hugged Janet and then Debbie. "Jim told me you encouraged him to help with the dinner. Which was marvelous, I might add. Beyond anything I could have hoped for."

"You know Jim. He didn't need much encouragement," Janet demurred.

"We had twenty-one people there. Twenty-one!" Kim exclaimed. "I'd figured on ten at most, but somehow the caterer was aware of our last-minute guests, and it was the best Thanksgiving ever. Mom was overwhelmed. Literally. But she hung in through it all and is holding court at Good Shepherd throughout the weekend. People are going to stop by and see her in a quiet setting before they all head out of town. She was so surprised."

Kim's report warmed Janet's heart. "I'm so glad it worked out for you."

"I wanted to stop over here first thing because I'll be visiting with family today too, although I'll be back for the afternoon and evening train runs. Did you know that when my niece's plane had to reroute to Cincinnati, Jim drove there and picked up her and her son? There wasn't a rental car to be had on Wednesday night, so he took it upon himself to make sure they got here in time."

"He's a good man."

"He sure is, and a great friend to my brothers. You should have heard the three of them talking about everything from being in the army to high school football prowess. Of course, they were *all* amazing, to hear them tell it."

"I expect they were." Debbie grinned. "Fish grow in size and strength every time we tell the story."

"True words. Did both of your brothers serve in Vietnam?" Janet asked.

Kim shook her head. "Marcus went to Vietnam as the war was ending. Neal went to Germany. Marcus said they suspected the withdrawal because orders began changing around then. He'd left college and been drafted, but his time overseas was short, and he was glad of it."

"What year was that?" Janet moved to her oversize bag and pulled out the mysterious letters.

"Seventy-one."

"And we know from the stamp that these letters were dated after '68, so that narrows things down if '71 is our potential cutoff year." Janet tapped the top envelope. "Our letter writer was careful about what he wrote, but he'd have to be if he was sent to the front."

"Which means he might have been one of the local boys to serve in Vietnam. He did say he wanted to come home. Several times."

"The blessing of a small town might work in our favor," Janet said. "You've got access to town notes about Korea and Vietnam, don't you, Kim?"

"Older stuff is still on microfiche, but I shifted a lot to digital access to make it easier to work with. Let me check that out. No luck with Abby Meyers?"

"Nothing we could follow up on." Janet left it at that because they'd agreed to let it go.

"If we don't find the person, at least we tried." Kim's phone pinged, and she read the screen with a smile. "It seems the family is getting ready to come over here for breakfast. Debbie, they'll all want your home fries. The Palmer boys like them nice and crisp, and there's a whole lot of Palmers who will be heading this way in about an hour."

"I'm on it."

Janet's phone rang as they were closing up shop that afternoon. She was startled to see the call was from Good Shepherd. She answered at once. "Hello?"

"Janet, it's Ashley at Good Shepherd."

"Ashley, how nice to hear from you. How was your Thanksgiving?"

"It was lovely. I actually worked here to give some others time off with their families. My mom was working too, so we're celebrating on Sunday."

"I'm glad, and it was good of you to give others that day off. What can I do for you?" Janet asked.

"One of our residents asked me to call you."

"Really? Who?"

"Miss Eidenbach."

That was the last name Janet had expected to hear. "Seriously?"

"Yes ma'am. She was wondering if you and Debbie could stop by."

"When?"

"Today if possible."

At that moment Janet thanked God for the blessing of Charla and Paulette because without them she'd have to say no. They were technically closed, but they had more baking to do. "How about half an hour from now?"

When Janet and Debbie parked, it was clear the Good Shepherd staff had been busy. Holiday lights sparkled in various rooms and on the trees outside. The groundskeepers would keep the trees lit through February, adding a bright and hopeful glow to the long nights of a northern winter.

Ashley waved them over as they came in the door. To their left, several members of Kim's family were visiting with Eileen. Ray Zink, another local World War II hero, had joined Eileen, Kim, and the out-of-town family in the cozy solarium. The conversation seemed joyous and lively.

Ashley motioned toward the hall of apartments. "Miss Eidenbach asked for you to come to her suite. Truth be told, I don't think anyone other than a doctor has ever been invited to her room. This is so out of character."

"We're happy to do whatever works for her," Janet said, and Debbie agreed.

They found Ann Marie's suite door halfway down the long hall. Janet lifted her hand to knock but then hesitated.

Debbie offered an understanding expression. "She reached out to us. I know we agreed to back off, but the circumstances have changed. This isn't us pushing her boundaries. This is her inviting us in."

Janet nodded, blew out a breath, and knocked.

Ann Marie swung the door open a few seconds later. She stood there for a moment as if second-guessing her decision then shifted to the side. "Come in."

The small apartment was as neat and tidy as a pin.

"We'll sit here." Ann Marie pointed to the small kitchen area.

Four chairs nestled around a table in perfect condition. A folding TV tray was set up beside the wide recliner. Salt and pepper shakers stood on the tray table. Janet surmised that the small woman took her meals there alone while watching TV. But then Harry Franklin often did the same thing. It was easier all around.

Ann Marie sat with her back to the armchair. She didn't beat around the bush at all. "Those letters."

Janet's heart skipped a beat, but she stayed quiet. Sometimes saying nothing was the best way to get a story told.

"They weren't mine." Ann Marie grimaced. "I took them a long time ago when I was young and stupid and pretending I was a different person. A person who was loved and cherished. Married. I shouldn't have, but I did it because every time Richard Chilson came into the post office before he went to war, my heart felt like it was on fire."

Janet exchanged a look of surprise and recognition with Debbie. Richard Chilson was the long-lost love of Winnie Gayle, the eccentric elderly woman who lived at Hummingbird Acres with her nephew and his family.

"He was so quiet. So humble. So good."

Janet was surprised at the tenderness in her voice. "We've heard the same things about him."

"Then he was gone, just like that, but when letters started coming, addressed to Winnie Gayle, I couldn't help myself. She couldn't love him like I did. She didn't understand him like I did. I was lonely, and so was he. I dreamed about that man every day, making up ridiculous stories in my head. When I went back later and reread those letters, I realized that I was a fool, a silly, lovesick girl who stole someone else's romance right out from under them. The whole thing stabbed me in the heart every time I saw Winnie sitting so lost and alone at the depot. Waiting for the man who loved her. The man who was never coming home."

Winnie Gayle had become a constant visitor on a bench outside the depot after Richard was killed in Vietnam. To make matters worse, their secret marriage had never been properly registered, so Winnie didn't even receive the widow's benefits that should have gone to her. Once her secrets were revealed, her nephew pushed the county to find the records and rectify the situation. When the government dragged its heels, Bobby Gayle had threatened to go straight to the media with the whole story. They came around quickly after that, and Winnie had received the benefits she deserved earlier that summer.

"I lived with the guilt for a long time." Ann Marie folded her hands tightly. "I went from being jealous of her to being disgusted with myself. That continued until today."

"Why today?" asked Debbie.

Ann Marie's expression turned thoughtful. "Pastor Nick held a service in the chapel here yesterday. I didn't go, but after the service he stopped by each and every room. He told me that he wanted to see everyone, whether they came to the service or not. He said that the people are the church, even if they're tucked away in a house or a set of rooms. He gave me such a look of warmth and understanding that I started to talk. Babble, even. Until I'd told him everything and then I started to bawl. I don't cry. Ever."

Her stern expression underscored her words, and Janet didn't doubt it for a moment.

"But I cried yesterday, and Pastor Nick told me how God forgives us. All of us. He told me to come clean and move on, so that's what I'm doing. I knew it the moment he said the words, and I already feel better telling you two about it. Anyway. That's my story. And I'm sorry. Real sorry," Ann Marie said. "If you can get those letters to Winnie, I'd be glad to put all this behind me. If you have time."

"Of course we have time," Janet said. "We're happy to do it. We're so glad you had Ashley call. It took a lot of courage for you to tell us this, but I'm glad you did." She stood. Something about the woman's character said she wasn't one to belabor things.

Debbie stood too. "Do you want us to say anything to Winnie on your behalf?"

Ann Marie swallowed hard. "Please tell her I'm sorry and I hope she can forgive me."

She didn't see them to the door. She stayed there in the kitchen chair, staring at the table.

They retraced their steps to the lobby, exited, and walked straight to the car. They got in, and Janet put the key in the ignition.

"Where to?" she asked, but she knew exactly where they were going.

"Hummingbird Acres, to right an old wrong," Debbie replied firmly. "As long as it's okay with Marcy. I'll call her and explain. We don't want to blindside Winnie without Marcy being aware. Then I'll text the others that we'll be later than expected. Dad already has the tent set up with Greg and your dad. Charla texted me while we were talking to Ann Marie to let me know that we have everything ready for Light Up the Town. Paulette and your mom can get things stocked outside if we miss the beginning of the event. The priority now is to fix this for Winnie."

Debbie put the call to Marcy on speaker. To say Marcy was amazed by the story was an understatement, but then she asked if Debbie and Janet could come straight over. "It's just me and Aunt Winnie here right now. Come right up to the house. News like this will be a shock to her, but I also know it will be a blessing. And to have a blessing at this time of year just makes it more special."

"We're on our way now," Janet said.

"We'll be here," Marcy replied, and Debbie disconnected the call.

As Janet turned south, away from town, Debbie texted their various helpers and read the answering texts out loud. "From your mother. 'We've got this. Not our first rodeo. We'll see you when you get back.'"

Janet grinned. "Sounds like Mom. And what did Greg say?"

"'Take as long as you need, sweetheart. I'll be here when you get back.'"

Janet hummed softly. "That's the kind of text that wins a girl's heart, isn't it?"

Debbie beamed at her. "It sure is."

# CHAPTER NINETEEN

The Gayles' sprawling barn was thoroughly decked out for Christmas and was home to a large group of various vendors. Lights emphasized the gambrel roof facing the road, and similar lights ran along the barn's long northern exposure. Smaller twinkle lights trimmed the covered "porch" area. Each of the six posts were wrapped in lighted garland. Weather-friendly red bows completed the look. Two vintage wheelbarrows had been filled with boughs of greenery then decked out with frosted pine cones and tiny twinkling lights.

It was beautiful. The large cooperative, a fairly new enterprise outside of town, was ready to welcome shoppers through the double glass doors, but Janet and Debbie didn't head for the barn today, per Marcy's instructions. They drove up to the house.

The temperature had dropped. The forecast predicted an encroaching winter storm. From the force of the wind as they walked up the porch steps, it seemed the forecast might be right.

Marcy opened the door as they came across the porch. "Come on in." She ushered them into the cozy living room and shut the door snugly. "It looks like we're going to get some significant winter weather, doesn't it? Maybe snow to brighten the lighting event?"

"Definitely cold enough for snow," Debbie agreed.

"Give me your jackets. I won't hear of you rushing off without at least a cider or an eggnog or something friendly," she told them.

"We don't want to take up too much of your time," Janet protested. "We know you're busy with the co-op."

"Nonsense. Claire's caught up on her course load, so I have a respite from work this evening. She'll close it up at six as usual, and she won't need me for that. Come on. Make yourselves comfortable."

Janet and Debbie obeyed, shrugging out of their jackets and hanging them on a nearby coatrack.

"Aunt Winnie will be right along." Marcy grinned. "And by 'right along,' I mean she'll get here in her own time. When I told her you were coming by, she informed me that she wasn't in suitable attire, and that it takes some effort to change things out. Her decisions aren't always based on weather or season but on the mood of the day."

"Does she know what mood she's likely to need to dress for?" Janet asked.

"No, I didn't mention why you were coming. Anticipation sometimes increases her anxiety, so I thought better of saying anything about the letters. Auntie's reactions to things keep life interesting around here, but I wouldn't have it any other way."

"I think you're a marvelous niece, and I'd love some eggnog." Janet sank into a cushy recliner covered with old-fashioned calico-style fabric. "And take no offense if I doze off. This chair is way too comfortable."

Marcy laughed. "Many an evening I've dozed off in that chair. My children take great pleasure in reminding me of my age. In turn, I remind them that if they got up when I do and did what I do all day, they'd nod off at eight o'clock too." She shared a smile with Debbie and Janet before she moved to the adjacent kitchen. "They probably wouldn't, of course, but it makes me feel good to think so."

She returned with the eggnog a few moments later. As she came through the kitchen, the back door opened.

Winnie Gayle swept in like a vintage movie heroine. Her long cloak swirled above the kitchen floor, and the hooded top covered her hair. She reached up with both hands and slipped the hood off, onto her shoulders. The dark green cloak was lined with an exquisite plaid in shades of blue, green, yellow, red, and black.

Janet complimented it right off. "Winnie, that cloak is gorgeous. The plaid is a beautiful blend of tones. I love it."

"It's the official tartan of Macleod of Harris," Winnie replied. "A nod to my true self, as it were. Marcy helped me research my roots on the internet. There's another Macleod tartan, you know." She lifted her chin in an almost royal gesture. "Lewis. But my heritage is of the Harris family, which is distinctly different."

"Is the cloak new?" No sooner had Janet posed the question than she realized her mistake.

Winnie sighed. "The modern tendency to make inquiries about one's possessions, one's clothing, and one's accessories and about purchase, price, or availability of a personal item is most disturbing. It is a tacky habit that seems to have grown in acceptance, but I urge you, Mrs. Shaw, to eschew it." She hung up the beautiful cloak and then crossed to a free recliner. "It is best to avoid the bad habits of the public in favor of more demure pursuits."

"Auntie, may I share what we found out concerning your lineage?" Marcy asked as she sat beside Debbie.

"Since these kind ladies were instrumental in helping right those old wrongs, they may certainly know what's been long hidden and only recently discovered," Winnie replied. "I'd like them to know what I long suspected. I was born into another family."

"Yes, we heard that." Janet beamed at Winnie.

"It was an odd circumstance to find myself in." Winnie sat upright, with her chin up and her shoulders back, much as she'd been described when she used to sit in waiting outside the depot long ago. "To have my past delved into in no small number of ways. I expected to find it most intrusive, but it was quite enlightening when all was said and done. Although we will probably never know exactly how it happened. Was I switched at birth purposely or inadvertently? Did some tragedy befall my birth parents and a kindly neighbor took me in? Or was I cast aside by an uncaring mother who preferred her own freedom to caring for an infant daughter?"

Janet couldn't imagine having any such questions about her own past, but she could see how Winnie might be able to enjoy the mystery.

"I may never have answers to those questions," Winnie continued. "I've resigned myself to that fate. Suffice it to say that I know I'm someone else. Who that person would have or could have been, we'll never know. But I am here now, with family—in a manner of speaking. Chosen family rather than blood. We have no idea whether my birth was recorded under another name or at all, or how my parents acquired my fraudulent papers, but it is an interesting state of affairs." She straightened and scooted to the edge of her seat. "Did you bring your famous doughnuts with you? I'm partial to them, as I'm sure you know."

"I'm sorry. We came straight here from another visit, so we don't have any treats with us," Janet said.

"Are you coming to the village for the lighting celebration tonight?" Debbie asked. "We plan to have them there."

Marcy shook her head. "Winter weather isn't good for Auntie."

Winnie gave an aggrieved sniff. "I'm not as fragile as all that. I've been through more winters than you have, young lady."

"I know, ma'am," Marcy said, patting her hand. "That means you've already paid your dues and shouldn't have to anymore."

"I'll come by with doughnuts after church tomorrow," Debbie promised. "If that works for you."

"I would be most obliged, thank you." Winnie offered Debbie a gracious nod. "So what brings you by today?"

Janet took the lead. "Winnie, we came to see you for a different reason today. A reason we stumbled on by complete accident, which involves your late husband. It's another mystery about your past, but separate from your heritage."

The reference to Richard Chilson softened the elderly woman's features. She toyed with the necklace she wore for a moment before speaking. "It is odd to have others speak of him in such a fashion with our union summarily dismissed by those in charge. He was here but then gone so quickly. So quietly. With no one knowing of our vows."

The elderly woman had carried that secret and her sadness quietly for over fifty years until a depot memory had helped bring things forward the year before.

"Not as quietly as you thought." Janet kept her voice soft. "These were found in a house undergoing renovation. They're yours,

Winnie." She handed over the bundle of letters. "They were misdirected a long time ago, but they've found their way home."

Winnie studied the envelopes then lifted her gaze to the other women. "What are these?"

"Open one," Debbie suggested.

Winnie opened the top envelope and slid out the folded sheet of paper. Then she straightened the page.

It took a moment before Winnie realized the treasure trove in her hands. When she did, her hands shook. So did her voice. "Letters? From Richard? But how? And why is our information crossed out on the envelope?"

Janet couldn't begin to come up with the right words to explain the situation.

Fortunately, Marcy saved her from needing to. "Auntie, sometimes we don't need to know all the answers. Sometimes it's better to just embrace the moment, as we have with your identity. It's more important that they're found after all this time than how they were lost to begin with."

Winnie gazed down at the letters, and her eyes filled. Then she drew a deep breath and swallowed hard. "You're correct, Marcy. I've prayed for so long, so very long, for a word, a message. Any contact at all, because I knew he loved me. I knew he would have stayed here at my side if it had been allowed, but he was a man who took his service seriously. He loved God, his country, and his family. I will cherish these at my leisure, and likely in private if it's all the same to you ladies." She refolded the one in her hand and tucked it back into the envelope. Always prepared, she withdrew a lace-trimmed handkerchief from the pocket of her dress and blotted her eyes.

Janet expected her to hurry off to her carriage house quarters on the other side of the farmhouse driveway, but she stayed with them until Janet and Debbie were ready to leave. It seemed Winnie had decided that she had already waited years for these missives, and a few more minutes wouldn't make much difference.

When Janet and Debbie rose, Winnie did too. First she hugged Janet, then Debbie, and last Marcy. Everyone knew that Winnie Gayle was not a hugger, but she embraced them all today. "Thank you," she told them, her tone revealing the fullness in her heart. "You've changed everything for me. More than I can ever express."

And Janet realized they had. It was visible in her face, in Marcy's smile, in the way Winnie clutched those precious letters in her hand.

They headed back to Dennison.

Janet relished being part of Winnie's new contentment. Witnessing the older woman's joy and knowing Ann Marie had found some peace were both marvelous things. Kim had been blessed with a true family Thanksgiving, and Richard Chilson's love letters had found their way home at long last. Janet and Ian had enjoyed a beautiful holiday with family, and Debbie had taken a giant leap forward in her relationship with Greg by hosting his family for Thanksgiving.

Yet she frowned as she steered into the parking lot filled with holiday cheer.

She wanted that kind of satisfaction for Dani and the rest of the Addison family. But after so many dead ends, she hadn't come up with answers, and she still had no idea how to make that happen.

# CHAPTER TWENTY

T he guys outdid themselves on this tent setup," Debbie observed as they hurried from the café. They'd brought extra warm clothing that morning to add before heading out into the plummeting temperatures.

"They sure did. Proximity to electric outlets sure is a handy thing to have when you're working in outdoor venues. How cute is all this?"

"Super cute," Debbie said.

The two fathers and Greg hadn't simply erected the heavy-duty tent Janet's father purchased the year before. They'd strung lights from corner to corner and along the front posts. Inside the tent, a sturdy folding table held big round containers of cocoa mix beside two industrial carafes of hot water. Alongside those were large bags of miniature marshmallows and half a dozen canisters of whipped cream.

Christmas-themed hot cups formed rows of color to one side, and chocolate chip cookies would be displayed in shallow wicker baskets on the other side of the front table. The baskets were lined with bright red plaid and trimmed in festive holiday bows that echoed the bigger bows at the front corners of the tent. The combination of lights, bows, and color gave their tent a grand Christmas effect in front of the holiday-themed depot. It was just what they had wanted.

Janet's and Debbie's fathers relaxed with Ian at the counter, enjoying a well-earned break. Greg had gone to take the boys to basketball practice. Paulette had cleaned the café and left, and Debbie had gone to briefly scope out the event while Janet's mother was handling what seemed to be an endless line for dollar cookies.

The café was technically closed, and dollar cookies weren't their normal fare. However, during the Christmas Train runs they'd decided to offer the cookies for a one-dollar donation. Each dollar collected went to the Salvation Army to commemorate its significant part in the Dennison Depot's history. It was their way of recognizing how thousands of people had cooperated to make a difference to so many troops eighty years before.

"This whole thing is catching on already." Ian took a spot beside Janet as she filled a mug with coffee. He indicated the groups of happy people clustering in the downtown area. "The town is filled with holiday spirit. Not the commercial type either. It's nice to see."

"It is," she agreed. "I'm so pleased with how everything has gone the past few weeks, Ian. I couldn't ask for more—except to figure out who's pestering the Addisons." She realized that she'd forgotten to fill him in about something. "Did I tell you that I saw a dark SUV that I think belongs to Charlie Briscoe pull out of the Christkindl Market yesterday, right behind Dani? As if he was following her."

Ian lifted a brow. "Remember our conversation about puzzles with extra pieces?"

She mulled that over while a mother settled her three children's squabble over cookie sizes. Then realization dawned. "Charlie isn't one of the suspects. He's the extra piece in the puzzle, the one that doesn't belong."

Ian laughed. "Because a guy might have a different reason for visiting a woman on occasion? Maybe more than weed control?"

"You knew." She glared at him. "How did you know, and why didn't you say anything?"

"Sworn to secrecy. They didn't want other people up in their business. You'll know that part soon enough. But yes, Charlie should be off the list. Permanently. Which leaves—" His words were cut off as both of their phones hummed notifications.

Ian had synchronized their phones with the trail cams. One angle went to Janet's phone. The next camera's image went to Ian's. They both opened their views to see someone unlocking the donkey pen gate and then opening it.

"Mack?" Janet squawked in surprise as the footage loaded, revealing several images of Mack Jankowski.

The supposedly friendly neighbor crept along the donkey pen, likely knowing the Addisons were setting up for the lighting festivities in the village. He peered around, unaware of the cameras trained on him. Then Janet saw him open the gate just wide enough for the donkeys to run free.

Ian radioed for backup and left at a run.

Debbie's mom came in as he went out, and Janet grabbed her arm. "Can you step in here with Mom? Just take their dollars and give them their cookies."

"Of course." Becca didn't hesitate. "Are you following Ian? Is it safe, sweetheart?"

Janet wasn't sure how to answer that, but she didn't have to.

Her dad and Vance left their stools and came her way. "She'll be fine. We'll go with her. Let's get moving, Janet." Once they were out of earshot, her dad added, "Where are we going?"

"Claymont Creek Farm, where it turns out that the nice neighbor, Mack, is the one who's been creating havoc for the Addisons. We have to hurry."

It was frustratingly slow going through the village as people gathered for the highly anticipated event. Fortunately, once they left the town limits, the roads were quieter. So was the farm when they reached it. The farm store closed earlier in November and December because the parking lot wasn't lighted. The Addisons didn't want anyone hurt in the dark.

It wasn't fully dark yet, but dusky shadows stretched from the far side of the farm, and the farm store had closed nearly an hour before, for which Janet was grateful.

Why on earth did their longtime neighbor want to make trouble for them? Janet had thought he liked the Addisons.

Janet's lights caught movement in the road ahead. The Addisons' miniature donkeys ran amok, with no idea of the danger they were in, frolicking down the road as night fell.

"Vance, you down for an old-fashioned roundup?" Dad asked.

"Let's do it," Debbie's father confirmed.

Janet pulled to the shoulder, and all three of them got out. The donkey enclosure wasn't far from the road, but the excitement of having three humans trying to corral them created a thrilling game of chase for the donkeys. Without halters or leads, they all dashed to and fro, eluding the novices' attempts to recapture them.

Then, like superheroes from an action movie, Dean and Brady Addison came their way from the donkey shed. Halters in hand, they approached the donkeys slowly and calmly, murmuring soothingly as if they had all the time in the world.

The maneuvers worked. Three of the donkeys paused. Their ears perked up when they heard Brady's voice, which they knew well, and they trotted toward him. They let him and Dean settle their halters into place and lead them into the enclosure, where Brady rewarded them with a basket of apple peelings. Dean carefully secured the gate once more.

"Brady." Janet hugged him and Dean when the donkeys were safely back where they belonged. "How did you know to come?"

"Ian called and asked us to head over quick because we needed to get the donkeys, make sure Mack ended up behind bars, and get back to the lighting-up ceremony before Dani noticed we were missing."

"Well, if we miss the official light-up time, the lights will still be on tomorrow night. And every night after that until New Year," Vance said.

Janet noticed that Dean and Brady exchanged a glance, but Ian's cruiser pulled up beside them before she could ask about it. Brendan's police car followed, with Mack Jankowski in the back.

Janet stepped closer to the car to study him.

Mack had appeared spry and cheerful when he'd sweet-talked them a few weeks before. Today he looked old, sad, and angry.

Brendan rolled down the window. "Are the donkeys okay?"

"They are, thank you. Dean and Brady got here. The donkeys know and trust Brady, so it was much easier after they arrived. I see you accomplished your task as well."

Brendan's smile vanished. "We sure did."

She turned to Mack. "I thought you were their friend, Mack. More importantly, *they* thought you were their friend. They're good people, and you've been neighbors for years. How could you?"

He scowled. "Clint made me a promise years ago when we had to pull out my orchard. The trees had gotten a bad blight. They had to be burned, and I didn't have the money to invest in new trees and fencing. Clint promised he'd do it, that he'd replant the orchard once the blight was out of the soil." Anguish underscored his rage. "I wanted my Rosie to be able to look out at trees again. She wouldn't have even cared what kind they were—she just loved that orchard. It broke her heart when we had to uproot the whole thing, and it broke mine to know she died without ever seeing it rebuilt."

In spite of herself, Janet felt for him, though she couldn't condone his behavior.

"Clint had the tools to reestablish. I didn't. He contracted the land for twenty years, which I thought was plenty of time to follow through on what he'd said." The elderly man almost choked on the words. "And he never planted one tree. Some wheat here and there and hay for those donkeys that screeched at me every time I came by."

Janet continued to hold her tongue.

"My wife deserved better than that. I deserved better than that. Now I've got an offer on my place, a good one, and I wanted Clint Addison to know how little I think of him. They're going to build a neighborhood at my place once the approvals go through, and Clint will lose over fifty tillable acres he's been renting from me. Let's see how he and his stupid farm do after that, eh?"

"You've been holding a grudge against Clint all this time?" Janet drew a breath. "Mack, did you ever ask Clint about it?"

Before he could answer, Dean chimed in. "If you had, he could have told you that the DEC examined your soil at his bidding, and it wasn't conducive to orcharding with today's trees. They recommended a site on the south side of the farm, and that's what Dani's planning to do. They were going to tell you later this winter when things slowed down. It took them a while to come up with the full plan they wanted to present to you."

Mack's scowl deepened. "The DEC doesn't run my farm, and the government doesn't get to tell me what to do with my own land. I wanted trees. Clint said he'd do it. He broke his word, and my wife died never seeing her trees again. Never seeing her grandkids run through the orchard like she wanted, picking apples, playing tag. And I blame Clint Addison for that. End of story."

There was no talking to him, Janet realized. He'd harbored so much anger and resentment that he couldn't rationalize what others said, because reason didn't matter. His anger and grief had overrun his good sense.

Ian came her way and put an arm around her shoulders and then shook hands with Dean and Brady. "You guys don't waste any time."

"Not when it comes to family," Dean replied stoutly.

"I'm glad to see that you've patched things up," Janet told him. "When did you find out about the DEC report?"

"When I was here to clear things up with Dad myself. He's always got his reasons, but he's terrible at communicating them," Dean said. "You have to have a blunt conversation with him, which doesn't occur to most of us to do. As soon as he realized that I felt taken advantage of, he apologized to me. Apparently, he took my refusal of money once as a permanent refusal, and he knew he'd be insulted if someone kept offering to pay him for work he wanted to do for free. So he never asked me again, and I don't like asking to be paid." He chuckled. "Two stubborn men locked in a miscommunication for months, simply because neither of us wanted to bring it up. Mom and Dani have given us plenty of grief over it, you can be sure."

"As long as you've mended things, that's what matters," Janet told him firmly.

He grinned at her. "That's what we've been saying, but you know how these Addison women are. We're going to hear about it at least as long as the conflict lasted, if not longer."

Brady checked the time on his phone. "We've got twenty minutes until the lighting, and it's a ten-minute drive. We should probably get moving."

"See you later." Ian made sure Janet got safely into her car with Vance and her father. He and Brendan were on patrol tonight, but Captain Hernandez had stayed on hand in town in case they got held up at the Addisons'. Janet was glad for that, since he'd provide an extra pair of hands while they got Mack processed at the station.

She drove back to town, reflecting on some deeply mixed feelings. On one hand, she was relieved that they finally had answers about the mysterious happenings at Claymont Creek Farm. But on the other hand, she doubted those answers would bring much peace to the Addisons, and her heart ached over that.

Their normal parking lot had filled up while they were gone, so Janet parked up the road and around the corner.

Ian startled her by meeting her at the booth.

"What are you doing here?" she asked. "Don't you have to do a ton of paperwork and then go back out on patrol?"

He grinned and took her hand. "It can wait until after."

"After what?"

He put a finger to his lips as the sound system clicked on. It had been installed for the new ice rink, but it wasn't the ice rink owner talking.

It wasn't the mayor either, to give his speech before they lit the town.

Instead, Charlie Briscoe spoke into the microphone. "Dani Addison, can they spare you from the fried-cake booth for a few minutes? It seems I was asked to have the first ice dance of the season with my choice of partners, and I can't think of anyone I'd rather share that honor with than you."

From her nearby booth, Dani gaped at him in shock and then sent a questioning look to her father.

Clint flashed her a broad smile and flapped a hand at her.

Dani rushed out of the booth toward Charlie.

The wind had picked up, tossing fluffy white flakes around as Dani crossed over to Charlie. The wind made her slide as she reached him, and Janet gasped, thinking she would fall.

But Charlie caught Dani and grinned. Then he spun her around. And when the opening notes of "Stairway to the Stars" played on the loudspeaker, Charlie Briscoe and Dani Addison danced.

Janet elbowed Ian. "You knew this was going to happen."

He laughed. "I sure did, and keeping the lid on it wasn't easy when you kept insisting Charlie was the primary suspect in the Great Farm-Pestering Caper."

"You could have told me."

He held up a hand. "Nope. Gave my word. Charlie wanted to surprise her."

"He's the anonymous donor for Light Up the Town too, isn't he?" she asked, finally able to put together the other puzzle. "Everyone thought it was Rick Radner, but they were wrong. This was Charlie's intention all along."

"I can neither confirm nor deny what I have been told in confidence. But I do know that whoever the donor is, he wanted to give a lovely gift to the town he loves. And that's exactly what he's done. He nailed it right down to the music. Charlie Briscoe's come home to stay, and everyone in this town should be glad that he did."

# CHAPTER TWENTY-ONE

"I can't imagine holding a grudge all that time. It must have festered and poisoned him from the inside for so many years." Debbie shook her head from her seat beside Greg on Janet and Ian's sofa three hours later. Greg had his arm around Debbie, and the image of two of her friends so happy pleased Janet as much as anything else.

The girls had headed back to college after the lighting festivities wound down. The fact that Tiffany would be back home in three short weeks for Christmas break made the goodbye easier than Janet had expected.

"What a waste of time and energy," Janet said. "And that pretty house and farm will be filled with more houses if the approvals go through. That's not necessarily a bad thing, but it will be a huge change. I still don't know how Rick Radner's argument with Charlie fits into the picture, though. What would they have to fight about?"

Ian answered her. "Rick heard that Charlie's initial attempts at farming hadn't gone well. He approached Charlie about a deal to let RDI develop the land. Charlie paid him a personal visit to make sure he understood that his family farm wasn't for sale. A few comments were taken the wrong way, and the conversation got more heated than it had to. But they've worked it out since then and are fast friends again. If things continue to progress between Charlie and Dani, the Addisons won't have to worry about losing the farmland they rented from Mack. I'm pretty sure a Briscoe/Addison merger would benefit both."

"You've always put things in the most romantic way, Ian," Debbie teased, and they all laughed.

Janet set bowls of popcorn on the coffee table then sank onto the love seat with Ian. "Romance under the stars—what a wonderful image. But what can we do to help poor Hailey? I don't like that she harasses people who are making an honest living. Still, it's hard to see a person who's already down on her luck get kicked around by rough circumstances."

"By the way, it was Mack that forced her off the road," Ian said. "He said he didn't know who it was at the time. He was in a hurry to get away from the area so that no one would suspect he'd released the hens."

"I expect the judge will make him pay reparations," Greg said.

"I think so too," Ian replied. "That will take a while, unfortunately. It's a good thing her sister was able to help her get a job once she heard how things have been going for her. Apparently, Hailey's been out of work for a while, and she fell in with the wrong crowd, who convinced her that protesting for animals was more important than finding work. But her sister has had a talk with her and is even loaning her a car while she waits on her settlement. She'll have a way to get back and forth to work once she heals."

"And I told her I'd stop by next week if the weather doesn't get too bad. I figured I'd take care of some of those repairs Debbie mentioned," Greg added. "If we start a kindness campaign, she might hop on board. Maybe it will calm down her angst to put her efforts toward more worthy causes."

Debbie beamed at him. "That was a wonderful thing to do, Greg Connor."

"No big deal." He shrugged his free shoulder. "Most folks could use a little help now and again, right? Especially at Christmas." He grabbed a bowl of popcorn and popped a handful into his mouth. "This is way better than movie popcorn. Whatever you did, you did it right."

"It's Ian's specialty, but it's also a family secret," Janet said.

Ian laughed. "It is not, but it could land you the heart of a good woman, Greg."

"In that case, I'll definitely need the recipe," Greg said, smiling at Debbie, who flushed.

Ian settled his arm around Janet's shoulders and lifted his glass of eggnog in the air. "To us, all of us, and to many nights together around this fire."

"And other fires as well." Greg raised his glass too. "And speaking of fires, next year we're putting a big heater in that tent. Don't argue, Debbie. I already ordered it. Keeping you two warm is part of our job, and I take my jobs and my family seriously."

Debbie smiled up at him. "I wasn't going to object."

"No?" He gave her a dubious expression.

"Nope. I was just going to thank you. A heater would be marvelous. I kind of like being cared for, Greg. It's nice."

As they looked at each other, Janet was sure that her best Christmas present that year would be seeing her best friend so very happy. Nothing could be better than that.

Dear Readers,

It was an absolute pleasure to write a story about a busy farm in the height of the fall selling season.

My husband, Dave, and I started a pumpkin farm nine years ago as our retirement project, and it has taken on a life of its own! We never expected it to grow so quickly. In fact, the first two years of growing normal, everyday veggies were a complete and costly failure. But then our daughter advised us to focus on pumpkins and fall because it was so expensive to take kids to other fall farms. And then a sweet customer asked us if we could grow blue pumpkins.

I'd never heard of blue pumpkins, which are an Australian blend of Hubbard and Cinderella-style pumpkins, one of the most favored squashes on the planet.

We started with blue, white, and orange pumpkins. That was six years ago. Now we grow over seventy varieties of squashes and pumpkins, as well as hay bales and cornstalks.

It's an unbelievable adventure, so being able to put part of that fun—and include miniature donkeys—into a story was the best thing ever!

But the best part of this adventure is you. The people. The customers. The folks making a stop here a yearly tradition, babies in pictures from our first years who are now going off to kindergarten.

I hope you loved the joy of this mystery. I hope you embraced the holiday feel and getting to know Dennison, Ohio, a town working to remake itself even as we write books about it.

It is so much fun to be part of the series and part of watching this historic town's beautiful renewal. Wishing you the very best holidays this year and every year! God bless you!

Ruthy

# ABOUT the AUTHOR

**B**estselling, multi-published inspirational author Ruth Logan Herne has published over seventy novels and novellas. She is living her dream of being a published author, and in her spare time she is co-owner of a rapidly growing pumpkin farm in Hilton, New York. She is the baker-in-residence, the official grower-of-the-mums, and a true people person, so filling her yard with hundreds of people every day throughout fall is just plain fun!

She loves God, her family, her country, dogs, coffee, and chocolate. The proud mother of six with a seventh daughter of her heart and fourteen grandkids, Ruthy lives in an atmosphere where all are welcome, no mess is too big it can't be cleaned up, and food is shared.

# TRUTH BEHIND the FICTION

This story gave me the perfect opportunity to finish up the decades-old mysteries surrounding the eccentric Winnie Gayle. Considered a bit spacy by family and friends, the artistic and dramatic woman lived her life believing she was in the wrong place and with the wrong family. Having grown up in a struggling family, Winnie often expressed the thought that she was more likely a princess than a pauper.

She grew up with a hint of disconnect from her family, partially of her own doing and partially because it turns out she was, in fact, given to the Gayles to raise at some point in time. DNA testing proved her suspicions. Now in her late seventies, there's not much Winnie can do about it, and no one matching her DNA came up on the ancestry search website. To her fictional credit, Winnie realized that knowing she was right was enough for now.

While a common fictional plot in TV, movies, and books, not many babies get switched at birth. Hospitals take great measures to make sure they have enough identifiers to be certain the right baby is going to the right home, yet it still happens occasionally. The wonders of DNA testing have cleared up many unsolved mysteries, not only of felonious crimes but also innocent mistakes in a hospital nursery.

DNA testing has opened a world that will help cure illness, thwart disease, prove innocence or guilt, and identify genetically

.linked people. It's a side of science that didn't exist twenty-five years ago and now seems commonplace, doesn't it? And yet, the first successful human gene map was completed in 2003 by members of the Human Genome Project, an international collaboration of scientists mapping out tiny parts of a whole. It took thirteen years to complete the effort, and it's been fine-tuned repeatedly since then. Now we treat it with the ease of flipping a light switch, but we know it took Edison a long, long time to get the final product right. And by doing so he changed the world.

# FROM the HOME-FRONT KITCHEN

## Decadent Southern Pecan Pie

This amazing pie became a hometown favorite when Janet made it at the Third Street Bakery. It's still a big draw at the Whistle Stop Café. The secret to its perfect blend of taste and texture is simple and marvelous: the sugar and corn syrup is lightly boiled together for two or three minutes then cooled a bit before whisking in the eggs.

Janet uses room-temperature eggs for good reason: Cold eggs tend to firm up the sugared syrup mix quickly, making it difficult to blend, so let your eggs hang out on the counter for about half an hour before you use them.

**Ingredients:**

1 cup sugar

1½ cups corn syrup

4 eggs (beaten in separate bowl)

¼ cup butter

1½ teaspoons vanilla

1½ cups coarsely chopped pecans

1 9-inch deep-dish pie shell, unbaked

**Directions:**

On stovetop, boil sugar and corn syrup together for 2 to 3 minutes. Let cool for about 5 minutes. Then whisk cooled syrup mix into 4 beaten eggs. Whisk quickly. Strain through small colander if lumpy. Add in butter, vanilla, and pecan pieces. Pour into unbaked pie shell and bake at 350 degrees for 45 to 60 minutes or until center is set.

*Read on for a sneak peek of another exciting book in the* Whistle Stop Café Mysteries *series!*

# WINTER WEATHER

## BY JENELLE HOVDE

Rome, Italy
December 1, 1943

*Inside the police station, Nico Carosi took a shuddering breath as he studied the stolen paintings spread haphazardly over the table. The frames were splintered and chipped, suggesting that the art had been pried off the walls as if it had resisted the act of violence to the bitter end. Art ripped from Jewish families or Italian aristocracy who openly defied Mussolini.*

*Nico swallowed hard, his mouth dry, as he glanced at the nearest piece. His hand hovered over the aged paper curling at the ends, yet he dared not touch the masterful lines of a weeping father clasping his adult son.* The Return of the Prodigal Son *by Rembrandt.*

*Someone had been careless this time. The paper bore evidence of a fresh tear. There was a splash on the left corner, staining the paper brown, as if by a stray teardrop. There was a wrinkle too, as if someone had grasped it to ward off its inevitable removal.*

*He flinched. Who had owned this piece, and where were they now?*

*"Well?" a sharp nasal voice demanded. "How much is it worth?"*

*He whirled around to see the captain staring at him. The man's oiled black mustache twitched.*

*Nico exhaled slowly. He was indeed an artist, hired to paint monstrosities for his country—or rather, propaganda posters. He was also called in to assess any pieces taken "for the good of the Italian empire." The new Roman Empire intended to rival any former Caesar's rule.*

*"It's worth a great deal. How much, I don't know yet. But one of your—"* He bit his tongue to keep from saying his thoughts out loud. One of your goons. *He cleared his throat. "One of your men ripped the sketch, and I cannot fix it."*

*The captain uttered an exasperated sigh as he prowled toward Nico. With the precise click of his* polished boots, he halted beside Nico, close enough to press against Nico's shoulder as if they were friends.

Nico suppressed a shudder at the captain's proximity. The black uniform with silver trim made Nico feel lightheaded with fear.

"I assumed it was a Rembrandt sketch," the captain said with a pompous sniff as he eyed the aged paper with his hands clasped behind his back. "The old woman swore it wasn't and tried to take it back. Do not blame my men for the damage. I have my orders to retrieve anything of value. Everything belongs to Mussolini, especially now that he has returned to power and will deal with any remaining traitors. As you well know, the state demands the immediate return of any historic Italian treasure."

A woman then. Rich once and still deserving of dignity. Perhaps someone like Nico's white-haired nonna, who used to slip him a small basket of cannoli when sugar and cream had been plentiful.

Nico's hands curled into tight fists at his sides. He forced his fingers to relax and slipped his hand into his pocket, fingering the blunt pencil stub tucked inside. His mind swirled with questions about the fate of the sketch's owner, but it would do no good to ask. Mussolini, after a failed coup, had exacted a terrible revenge on the country, including his own son-in-law, and Captain Accardo was Mussolini's man through and through. The authorities would not tolerate impertinent questions this season.

Nico moved to the next table, examining a small marble bust of a woman. Her cheeks were smooth and round. Like Sophia's.

But he would not think of Sophia at this moment. Could not, when six guards and their captain watched his every move. Any hint of a vulnerability such as affection could prove fatal for him as well as the object of those affections.

"This is more modern, I think, but in the style of ancient Greece." He removed his hand from his pocket and picked up the sculpture, noting the signature beneath the bust. "It's by Adolfo Wildt, an Italian artist. You can commission his work even now. I studied with Wildt three years ago."

"I assumed it was much older." The captain bristled, his cheeks flushing as Nico placed the bust back on the table. "I suppose I will need to dispose of it if it has no value."

"On the contrary, the bust is worth something," Nico replied softly. He kept his tone even. Any eagerness would betray his anxiety to save precious artworks like the sculpture, and they would destroy it for that alone. "Wildt is well respected."

Ten years before, several artists had banded together, envisioning another renaissance of expression. Il Secondo Futurismo, *Second Futurism*. Unlike Hitler, Mussolini had claimed to envision a world of art that allowed different styles to flourish, particularly those that echoed ancient Greece and Rome. But the promise of freedom of expression had been a lie, like every one of Mussolini's other lies about peace and prosperity and justice.

Nico moved to another table but stopped when the captain snatched his arm, hard fingers digging into flesh.

"You do not wish me to assess these?" Nico gestured to the vibrant painting resting against the table.

"Those are to be burned. Filthy pieces painted by *the* resistenza."

The cubist painting, stacked with several others, practically glowed with geometric red and orange, with each stroke slashed across the canvas as if rage had propelled the paintbrush. Yet the image was simple to discern as Rome on fire. The symbolic image repulsed Nico too, but perhaps not for the same reasons as the captain. He knew of his fellow artists, who had painted caricatures of Mussolini during the leader's arrest and paid the price. Such defiance. Such boldness. Did these artists now languish in a jail or a camp reserved for dissidents? Or worse?

He averted his gaze from the riot of angry colors, pulling his arm free of the captain's grip. "Then it appears my work here is done."

"You will, of course, bring your latest posters to me for review." The captain brushed a finger against his mustache as if he managed the finest of museums.

"In two weeks' time," Nico replied. He hated the posters commissioned to recruit more men for the war effort, especially now that German troops had rescued Mussolini from his recent captivity.

The resistance had attempted a coup back in September and failed. Allies pushed into Sicily and advanced further into Italy while Rome crawled with SS guards. Now, Nico painted to remind the Roman populace of the "illustrious future," should they stay the course. The latest prints comprised monstrosities of angular lines meant to mimic the fierce Roman gods. What good did such art do when children went hungry and women and men felt the weight of a ruthless government?

"You will do it sooner." The captain's demand fell over the hushed room while the uniformed men continued to watch Nico with suspicion.

He nodded once before exiting the storage room of the police station, a place meant for justice, not robbery.

*But Mussolini's secret police, the OVRA, or Organization for Vigilance and Repression of Anti-Fascism, saw no irony in their actions. They kept files on over 130,000 residents, focusing on Rome but with tightening control sweeping across the country at Hitler's insistence.*

*Nico straightened his coat, preparing for the bitter wind outside the station, which brought a few rare flakes of snow. He might even have enjoyed the first sign of winter weather if not for the low voices murmuring from the storage room.*

*"The chief of police has ordered another sweep of the area tonight," the captain muttered to the other men.*

*Nico paused in the dingy hallway, not daring to breathe so he could hear the rest of the speech. Yet what could he do? A shiver rippled through him at the mention of the chief of the secret police. Matteo Verga. Nico knew him better than he might have wished.*

*"Arrest anyone caught with the resistenza and anyone Jewish, or we will answer to the chief of police," the captain ordered from the storage room.*

*Fidgeting with his scarf, Nico paused longer than he ought, hoping to hear who might be the next target. No one deserved to fall into the hands of his old schoolmate, Verga. But as Nico fiddled with his coat on the pretense of buttoning it up, one policeman headed* toward the open door, grinding to a halt when his dark gaze collided with Nico's. The policeman narrowed his eyes in a silent threat.

Nico fled the station, pushing on the door to escape into the approaching night. The sky above lay like an iron curtain, dark and foul. He tugged up the collar of his coat as he rushed down the familiar streets until at last he found a cobblestone lane lined with shops closing for the night.

Dare he pray for the safety of the next victims? Or would God refuse to listen, as He usually seemed to these days? Did miracles exist anywhere during this Christmas season?

Nico found no answer as the wind continued to whip through the street and the meager sunlight faded into twilight. He hurried toward his home, a small flat with the living room that served as a studio, right above a struggling leather goods store.

To his left, the scent of fresh bread lingered in the air, a siren call that caused his stomach to rumble loudly. Plunging a hand through his hair, Nico stopped in front of a glass window covered with the smudged fingerprints of hungry children.

The Giudice Bakery. He peered into the shadowy depths, looking for her. But only his gaunt reflection, replete with wild dark curls, stared back at him.

Yet he waited all the same for a single glimpse of Sophia Giudice, who in better days had helped her father, Angelo, stock the loaves and set out trays of sugar-coated chiacchiere—*fried angel wings—crispy cannoli oozing with vanilla cream, or buttery Italian wedding cookies that melted in his mouth. Treats now reserved for Hitler's best men.*

When Nico earned extra money from the posters, he worked up enough courage to purchase her biscotti. However, during his last visit, the taste of the hard cookie studded with pistachio nuts had turned to ash when Sophia had cast a baleful glance in his direction after one officer had complimented Nico's mural in the nearest gymnasium.

The shop appeared silent and shadowed this evening, perhaps closed while Nico had examined the stolen paintings on behalf of the regime. Giudice served everyone, but the average Italian could hardly afford anything but rice these days. The officers, on the other hand, often came to the bakery to buy the white bread, even as they sneered in disdain at the baker. Nico suspected Sophia hated them.

Perhaps she hated him too, and how could he blame her?

His throat tightened as he pushed away from the glass and trudged up the narrow stairs to his flat. He unlocked the door, eased out of his threadbare jacket, and slung it across the nearest chair. The apartment appeared extra dreary this Christmas season. He fumbled for a match and struck it, listening to the hiss as it flared to life. After lighting the gas lamp, he sank down onto the kitchen chair, more miserable than he could remember ever being. All around the cramped room, posters in bright red and black, now dry, hung about the walls, screaming for his attention. He couldn't escape the Fascist party if he tried. Hadn't his older brother warned him to leave Italy back in the thirties, before it was too late?

Now Alberto lived in America, no doubt running a restaurant with a pretty wife and plenty of children. Why had he and Alberto fought over where home was? Why hadn't his brother stayed in Rome to help him look after their aging nonna? Surely anyone could understand that Nico could never leave the city if their grandmother refused to abandon her beloved home. Yet now she was gone too, leaving him alone in the flat. Alone and trapped.

What a shame to let the months slip into years, with nothing but silence stretching between him and his remaining family. Nico dragged a palm across his face. Despite the memory of his nonna's voice reminding him to find something to be thankful for, the joy of

Christmas was nowhere to be found in his spirit. Years later, he still missed Alberto's ready smile and equally ready advice.

Was he destined to be alone forever? Nico's eyes watered as endless regrets suffused him.

Yet one small painting waited on the easel, the soft colors soothing against the red and black posters. His sole act of rebellion. The Madonna cradled the Christ child and stared back at him with luminous eyes, while the faint light of the star lined her hair and face with silver. A painting of hope and joy. Of tenderness.

He could almost imagine her whisper, "You carry such a heavy burden, Nico. Lay it down."

And so he did his best, choosing to lose himself in rich indigo and celestial silver. He picked up the nearest brush, the bristles stiff despite the recent cleaning, and reached for his oil paints.

His hand froze as a frantic knock sounded on the front door.

# A NOTE FROM the EDITORS

We hope you enjoyed another exciting volume in the Whistle Stop Café Mysteries series, published by Guideposts. For over seventy-five years, Guideposts, a nonprofit organization, has been driven by a vision of a world filled with hope. We aspire to be the voice of a trusted friend, a friend who makes you feel more hopeful and connected.

By making a purchase from Guideposts, you join our community in touching millions of lives, inspiring them to believe that all things are possible through faith, hope, and prayer. Your continued support allows us to provide uplifting resources to those in need. Whether through our communities, websites, apps, or publications, we inspire our audiences, bring them together, and comfort, uplift, entertain, and guide them. Visit us at guideposts.org to learn more.

We would love to hear from you. Write us at Guideposts, P.O. Box 5815, Harlan, Iowa 51593 or call us at (800) 932-2145. Did you love *Stairway to the Stars*? Leave a review for this product on guideposts.org/shop. Your feedback helps others in our community find relevant products.

*Find inspiration, find faith, find Guideposts.*

# Shop our best sellers and favorites at
# **guideposts.org/shop**

Or scan the QR code to go directly to our Shop

**While you are waiting for the next fascinating story
in the Whistle Stop Café Mysteries, check out
some other Guideposts mystery series!**

# SECRETS FROM
# GRANDMA'S ATTIC

Life is recorded not only in decades or years, but in events and memories that form the fabric of our being. Follow Tracy Doyle, Amy Allen, and Robin Davisson, the granddaughters of the recently deceased centenarian, Pearl Allen, as they explore the treasures found in the attic of Grandma Pearl's Victorian home, nestled near the banks of the Mississippi in Canton, Missouri. Not only do Pearl's descendants uncover a long-buried mystery at every attic exploration, they also discover their grandmother's legacy of deep, abiding faith, which has shaped and guided their family through the years. These uncovered Secrets from Grandma's Attic reveal stories of faith, redemption, and second chances that capture your heart long after you turn the last page.

*History Lost and Found*
*The Art of Deception*
*Testament to a Patriot*
*Buttoned Up*

*Pearl of Great Price*
*Hidden Riches*
*Movers and Shakers*
*The Eye of the Cat*
*Refined by Fire*
*The Prince and the Popper*
*Something Shady*
*Duel Threat*
*A Royal Tea*
*The Heart of a Hero*
*Fractured Beauty*
*A Shadowy Past*
*In Its Time*
*Nothing Gold Can Stay*
*The Cameo Clue*
*Veiled Intentions*
*Turn Back the Dial*
*A Marathon of Kindness*
*A Thief in the Night*
*Coming Home*

# SAVANNAH SECRETS

Welcome to Savannah, Georgia, a picture-perfect Southern city known for its manicured parks, moss-covered oaks, and antebellum architecture. Walk down one of the cobblestone streets, and you'll come upon Magnolia Investigations. It is here where two friends have joined forces to unravel some of Savannah's deepest secrets. Tag along as clues are exposed, red herrings discarded, and thrilling surprises revealed. Find inspiration in the special bond between Meredith Bellefontaine and Julia Foley. Cheer the friends on as they listen to their hearts and rely on their faith to solve each new case that comes their way.

*The Hidden Gate*
*A Fallen Petal*
*Double Trouble*
*Whispering Bells*
*Where Time Stood Still*
*The Weight of Years*
*Willful Transgressions*
*Season's Meetings*
*Southern Fried Secrets*
*The Greatest of These*
*Patterns of Deception*

*The Waving Girl*
*Beneath a Dragon Moon*
*Garden Variety Crimes*
*Meant for Good*
*A Bone to Pick*
*Honeybees & Legacies*
*True Grits*
*Sapphire Secret*
*Jingle Bell Heist*
*Buried Secrets*
*A Puzzle of Pearls*
*Facing the Facts*
*Resurrecting Trouble*
*Forever and a Day*

# MYSTERIES of MARTHA'S VINEYARD

Priscilla Latham Grant has inherited a lighthouse! So with not much more than a strong will and a sore heart, the recent widow says goodbye to her lifelong Kansas home and heads to the quaint and historic island of Martha's Vineyard, Massachusetts. There, she comes face-to-face with adventures, which include her trusty canine friend, Jake, three delightful cousins she didn't know she had, and Gerald O'Bannon, a handsome Coast Guard captain—plus head-scratching mysteries that crop up with surprising regularity.

*A Light in the Darkness*
*Like a Fish Out of Water*
*Adrift*
*Maiden of the Mist*
*Making Waves*
*Don't Rock the Boat*
*A Port in the Storm*
*Thicker Than Water*
*Swept Away*
*Bridge Over Troubled Waters*
*Smoke on the Water*
*Shifting Sands*
*Shark Bait*
*Seascape in Shadows*

*Storm Tide*
*Water Flows Uphill*
*Catch of the Day*
*Beyond the Sea*
*Wider Than an Ocean*
*Sheeps Passing in the Night*
*Sail Away Home*
*Waves of Doubt*
*Lifeline*
*Flotsam & Jetsam*
*Just Over the Horizon*

# Find more inspiring stories in these best-loved Guideposts fiction series!

## *Mysteries of Lancaster County*

Follow the Classen sisters as they unravel clues and uncover hidden secrets in Mysteries of Lancaster County. As you get to know these women and their friends, you'll see how God brings each of them together for a fresh start in life.

## *Secrets of Wayfarers Inn*

Retired schoolteachers find themselves owners of an old warehouse-turned-inn that is filled with hidden passages, buried secrets, and stunning surprises that will set them on a course to puzzling mysteries from the Underground Railroad.

## *Tearoom Mysteries Series*

Mix one stately Victorian home, a charming lakeside town in Maine, and two adventurous cousins with a passion for tea and hospitality. Add a large scoop of intriguing mystery, and sprinkle generously with faith, family, and friends, and you have the recipe for *Tearoom Mysteries*.

## *Ordinary Women of the Bible*

Richly imagined stories—based on facts from the Bible—have all the plot twists and suspense of a great mystery, while bringing you fascinating insights on what it was like to be a woman living in the ancient world.

## To learn more about these books, visit Guideposts.org/Shop